BALZAC AND HIS READER

Portrait de Balzac en robe de chambre, painted by Louis Boulanger (1836), reproduced courtesy of Musée des Beaux-Arts, Tours. Photo: Arsicaud, Tours.

BALZAC AND HIS READER

A Study of the Creation of Meaning
in *La Comédie humaine*

Mary Susan McCarthy

University of Missouri Press
Columbia & London, 1982

Library of Congress Cataloging in Publication Data

McCarthy, Mary Susan, 1949–
Balzac and His Reader.

Bibliography: p.
Includes index.
1. Balzac, Honoré de, 1799–1850.
Comédie humaine. I. Title.
PQ2159.C72M35   843'.7   82–2667
ISBN 0–8262–0378–7   AACR2

To my parents,
for years of love
and example

PREFACE

Several narrative strategies within *La Comédie humaine* incorporate into the narration the subjective response of the reader. Even as these techniques mold our reading of Balzac's work, they yield to the activity by which we participate with the author in the creation of a fictional universe. The focus of this study, then, is not only upon the nature of the transactions between author and text and between reader and text, but also upon the text itself, where we find evidence of the ultimate transaction formed by literature, between author and reader.

The merging of interests in *La Comédie humaine* and contemporary narrative theory raised several persistent questions: By what means did Balzac acknowledge and accommodate his readers, indeed feature them within his narrations? What is the relationship between Balzac's well-known concern for the reception of his fiction and his experimentation with the novel as an art form? Finally, by what literary techniques does the author communicate to us our function, at once shaping the form our reading will take and allowing us the interpretive freedom essential to a pleasurable reading?

It was, of course, impossible to treat the entirety of Balzac's work using the close textual analysis required by this study. It was equally impossible to identify every narrative strategy that relates reader to text. I resolved, therefore, to examine some of the most significant strategies: specific features or techniques found within single narrations (metaphor and description); the structure of a short story; and, finally, *La Comédie humaine* as a whole through its main unifying feature, the reappearing character.

I hope that both my methodology and conclusions will illuminate heretofore unexplored aspects of Balzac's work and will offer us new insights into the author as artist and craftsman, as well as into ourselves as readers. It is but the result of the continued appreciation and constant sense of discovery that are a part of reading *La Comédie humaine.*

BALZAC AND HIS READER

My interest in Balzac's work and in the reader's role in coproduction was first encouraged by Lorin A. Uffenbeck of the University of Wisconsin. I wish to extend sincere thanks to him here for his continued guidance and enthusiasm. I would also like to thank Victor Brombert, at whose urging, while I spent a summer working at Princeton University and subsequently, I completed a large portion of this project. I am grateful as well to Hope College for its financial backing during the summers of 1978 and 1980, during which time I was able to work without interruption. Finally, my warmest thanks to my husband, Joseph F. Byrnes, who listened, read, listened again, and responded to this material, and whose gentle support I have always felt and always appreciated.

I have quoted directly from five modern English translations of Balzac's works. They are, in order of appearance, *Ferragus*, "La Grande Bretèche," *Père Goriot, Lost Illusions*, and *A Study in Feminine Psychology*. For those works not recently translated, I have adapted older translations, relying heavily on the following:

> *The Rise and Fall of César Birotteau*, trans. Katharine Prescott Wormeley (Boston: Hardy, Pratt & Co., 1886).
> *The Quest of the Absolute*, trans. Ellen Marriage (Philadelphia: The Gebbie Publishing Co., 1899).
> *The Muse of the Department*, trans. Ellen Marriage and James Waring (Philadelphia: Avil Publishing Co., 1901).
> *A Double Family*, trans. William Walton (Philadelphia: George Barrie's Sons, 1897).
> *The Deserted Woman*, trans. Ellen Marriage (Philadelphia: Avil Publishing Co., 1901).
> *Albert Savarus*, trans. Katharine Prescott Wormeley (Boston: Hardy, Pratt & Co., 1892–1896).
> *Esther Happy*, trans. James Waring (Philadelphia: Avil Publishing Co., 1901).
> *The End of Bad Roads*, trans. Ellery Sedwick (Philadelphia: George Barrie's Sons, 1895).
> *Another Study of Woman*, trans. William Walton (Philadelphia: George Barrie's Sons, 1897).

Translations unless otherwise indicated are my own.

M.S.M.
August 1982, Stillwater, Oklahoma

CONTENTS

I

INTRODUCTION

C'est toujours à cause de la manière dont
une histoire est racontée que nous nous y
intéressons. Chaque sujet a sa forme spéciale.

(It is always because of the way in which
a story is told that we are interested in it.
Every subject has its own special form.)

Balzac, "Lettres sur la littérature"

Our image of Balzac as an artist has been much influenced
by the copious correspondence through which we glimpse
the artist at work. From his many letters, and of course the
works themselves, we have constructed an image of the frenetic worker, the author driven by a sense of his art, by debt,
and by need and at the same time propelled by a vision of a
masterwork. Although his was a grandiose plan for the historical portrayal of his own time, his vision was as much artistic
as it was historical. His letters and critical writing portray an
intense awareness of craft, the self-consciousness of the creative artist. As Balzac states in the "Avant-Propos" to *La
Comédie humaine*, the task of writing history in a literary
form was more difficult than the "simple" writing of history.[1]
History and artistry came together naturally and smoothly
for the author as his own description of his vision demonstrates.

En dressant l'inventaire des vices et des vertus, en rassemblant
les principaux faits des passions, en peignant les caractères, en
choisissant les événements principaux de la Société, en composant
des types par la réunion des traits de plusieurs caractères homogènes,
peut-être pouvais-je arriver à écrire l'histoire oubliée par tant
d'historiens, celle des moeurs. (1:11)

[In preparing an inventory of vices and virtues, assembling the facts of emotions, portraying character, selecting Society's important events, constructing models with the traits of several homogeneous personalities, perhaps I can write the history that is forgotten by so many historians, that of manners.]

Although he begins on a note of objectivity, as if he were, as he claimed to be, simply the recorder of an era, his description points to a consciousness of craft and of art within his work and a preview of the creativity at the heart of *La Comédie humaine*. He sought both in and through his writing the "sens caché," the hidden reality of society, the most profound meanings and motivations within the actions of its members. The search was both the privilege and the responsibility of the artist. "Le talent [de l'auteur] éclate dans la peinture des causes qui engendrent les faits, dans les mystères du coeur humain dont les mouvements sont négligés par les historiens"[2] ("An author's talent bursts forth in the portrayal of causes that produce the facts, in the mysteries of the human heart, the movements of which are neglected by historians"). Thus, the world the author creates for us, his readers, is that of his day as he perceived it, as well as that which was beyond, within, behind the visible surface as he was able to divine or imagine it. It was a duality of nature, of the person, and of society, a duality at once material and spiritual, which he sought to explore through his writings and which has been much discussed by the critics.[3] We find the evidence of that exploration at every level of *La Comédie humaine*. In the "Préface de la Première Edition" (1838) Balzac wrote of *Histoire de la grandeur et de la décadence de César Birotteau*:

> Ce livre est le premier côté d'une médaille qui roulera dans toutes les sociétés, le revers est *La Maison Nucingen*. . . . Toute oeuvre comique est nécessairement bilatérale. L'écrivain, ce grand rapporteur de procès, doit mettre les adversaires face à face. Alceste, quoique lumineux par lui-même, reçoit son vrai jour de Philinte:
>
> "Si tanta licet componere parvis." (6:35)
>
> [This book is the first side of a coin present in all societies; the opposite side is *La Maison Nucingen*. . . . Every comic work is necessarily bilateral. The author, that recorder of process, must place adversaries face to face. Alceste, although luminous in his

own right, is seen in full light opposite Philinte:
"If it is permitted to compare such great things to such small.")

While the duality of the world became a subject implicit in much of Balzac's writing, his choice of the fictional mode implied for him a further dual relationship, that of the reader and the text, and it is his recognition of that relationship that is the topic of this study. The fictional universe he fashioned for us is of course a mixture of historical writing and artistic creation. A fictional reality, or, more correctly, our illusion of it, is the result not only of the objective portrayal of what Balzac so adroitly observed, not only of his subjective representation, but also of the strategies and devices upon which his narrations are built, of the complicated construction of the text on multiple levels of theme, structure, and stylistics. Only because of its artistic rendering are we able to participate in Balzac's fictional world. Only through art, and what it demands of us as recipients, can that world transcend the epoch, the culture, and the man that it reflects. It is the author's construction of the work, with careful attention to the pleasure and to the creativity of the reader, that permits us to become so thoroughly engaged in the fictional universe of *La Comédie humaine*. That construction and its relationship to the reader deserve our careful attention if we wish to understand more deeply our fascination with this literature.

That Balzac should have chosen the literary form for his representation of a historical moment and for his investigation of its most profound meanings reflects a number of assumptions. Although it is in part to state the obvious, it is important to consider these assumptions and their implications. Of course, the choice of the novel form implies a craft to be mastered and attended to. It implies representation not only through realistic portrayal, but also through the use of such artistic devices as symbols, metaphors, descriptions, hyperbole, or minimization. Balzac certainly exercised his poetic privilege in the evocation-creation of a universe, and, as his own definition cited above indicates, the creation of a fictional reality was not in the representation of that which one knew, but in the creative assembly, choice, and composition of aspects of that reality, and in the structuring of these aspects and others into narrative form.

Of course, the literary form also implies readers, not mere recipients of the narration but active participants in completing the meaning that the story begins. The textual strategies to be studied here are evidence of the healthy respect that Balzac had for the power and imagination of the reader. He criticized his contemporary E. Sue, who, as he put it, "[prenait] ses lecteurs pour des ignorants"[4] "([took] his readers for know-nothings").

There are in Balzac's correspondence frequent references to the reading public, frequent requests, especially to Mme Hanska and other women, for response, criticism, and reaction. We know that the response to Balzac's work during his lifetime was mixed and that he strove for a long time, despite later protestations, to please the readers of his own day.[5]

The nature of that reading public, however, is significant because it greatly influenced the shape of Balzac's texts. A widening distance between artist and audience forced writers of the nineteenth century to abstract their audience far more than did writers of an earlier age. Thus it is that Balzac and his contemporaries seem to us at times to have been confounded by an audience they did not understand. According to Christopher Prendergast,

> The "mysterious" nature of the public is not just a matter of a failure to discover the evidence or to elaborate adequate methods of research; it is rooted in the particular realities of the nineteenth century, where the anonymity of the reading public is of the essence. In earlier periods there is frequently a close relationship between artist and public; indeed many writers are directly acquainted with many members of an anyway severely restricted circle of readers. In the nineteenth century, however, that intimacy begins to disappear; the relationship between writer and reader tends to become a basically economic one, mediated by the workings of the market, that is, by something essentially impersonal.[6]

As the author's concept of reader becomes gradually more abstract, the strategies to accommodate that reader within a text must, we may assume, demand closer attention and more subtle treatment. Although Balzac did at times take himself as the model of the reader (in his discussions of Cooper and Stendhal, for example), he did indeed formulate his narrative strategies and theories with an abstracted notion of the reader in mind.

> La vérité littéraire consiste à choisir des faits et des caractères, à les élever à un point de vue d'où chacun les croie vrais en les apercevant, car chacun a son vrai particulier, et chacun doit reconnaître la teinte du sien dans la couleur générale du type présenté par le romancier.[7]

> (Literary truth requires that an author select facts and personalities and elevate them so that everyone, upon seeing them, believes them to be true. What is truthful is different for everyone, and each reader must recognize shades of his own truth in the general color of that which is presented as typical by the novelist.)

As this passage indicates, the work could be constructed in such a way that an author could reach individual readers, permitting them to play out their individuality while at the same time exerting a measure of control over each response. Balzac accommodated the unknown reader of his day, unknown in temperament and taste,[8] as well as readers such as ourselves, in part through the construction of the narration that clearly defined the role to be played by the reader. Displayed in Balzac's writing, there are strong efforts to situate the reader in relationship to the narration, to then invite an active participation in the production of literary meaning, and to communicate the nature of that participation through the numerous strategies laid within the text. When he praised Stendhal for his "magnifique croquis militaire" ("magnificent military sketch"), the battle of Waterloo scene of *La Chartreuse de Parme*, Balzac portrayed himself as one such active reader, guided and inspired in his reading by the author's skillful style.

> [M. Beyle] ne s'est pas jeté dans la peinture complète de la bataille de Waterloo, il l'a côtoyée sur les derrières de l'armée, il a donné deux ou trois épisodes de la déroute; mais si puissant a été son coup de pinceau, que l'esprit voit au-delà: l'oeil embrasse tout le champ de bataille et le grand désastre.[9]

> ([M. Beyle] did not attempt a complete portrayal of the battle of Waterloo. Instead he concentrated upon the rear of the army,

giving two or three episodes of the rout; but so powerful was his presentation that one imagines beyond it: the eye takes in the entire battlefield and the terrible disaster.)

Indeed, we find in the critical writings of Balzac a significant attention to the craft of writing. He was highly critical, to cite but one example, of the *feuilletonistes* (serial writers) who composed their works on a day-to-day basis and for whom an installment of a story would be influenced, if not dictated, by the audience response to its predecessor. "[T]ous ceux qui publient leurs ouvrages en feuilletons n'ont plus la liberté de la forme"[10] ("All those who publish their novels in installments forfeit the benefits of the form") wrote Balzac. Even those works Balzac himself published *en feuilletons* were written, if he was at all able, in their entirety before the presentation of the first installment.

More interesting, however, than his criticism of others is the image we receive of Balzac himself: an artist on the cutting edge of artistic invention.[11] Balzac realized that the novel was the genre on the rise, the genre in which innovation was possible. He was aware of the revolutionary nature of Walter Scott's fiction and set his goals high in his desire to better the master in the formation and development of the historical novel. As Martin Kanes has pointed out, Balzac "took the first steps toward the contemporary self-consciousness of fiction, toward the break-down of mimesis as the conscious and accepted mode of narration."[12]

The attention to the nature of the reader's participation in the work that Balzac's writing manifests may well have led him to approve of, if not to enhance, twentieth-century critical tendencies, in particular those of reception theory. Literary criticism that has in the recent past emphasized scientific methodology, objective truth, and interpretation of the text in isolation has more recently turned toward a recognition of the importance of the reader and the considerable subjectivity inherent in the act of reading. In so doing, it makes tacit admission that all criticism, despite its most sincere efforts to remain objective and scientific, is, to a degree, subjective. That simple proposal, which has generated no little controversy, acknowledges the liberty and diversity that criticism represents and must tolerate. Critics now recognize and accept that each reader experiences a given work differently at different times and that the experience of literature will always be subjective. For the purposes of this study it is necessary to analyze the nature of the literary text in relation to its readers and, indeed, to examine the act of reading itself.

When I. A. Richards was working on *Practical Criticism* he was acutely aware of the subjectivity of the reader.[13] Richards did not appreciate the diversity he found in reader response, but rather sought to correct what he perceived to be misreadings and to bring about a uniformity of response. Were Richards writing today, he would perhaps again be interested in correcting erroneous readings that stem from misunderstandings of language, form, or history. But the direction of contemporary criticism might have led him to a greater appreciation of the valid diversity of response that is the object of so much attention. In "The Subjective Paradigm in Science, Psychology and Criticism,"[14] critic David Bleich suggests that subjectivity is the paradigm to be found at the very foundation of our intellectual era. It replaces, for him, an objective paradigm that, as the basis of intellectual activity, permitted many to believe in the possibility of a totally objective truth as well as in those purely scientific and objective methods believed capable of leading us to the truth. As criticism has recognized the subjectivity involved in the process of evaluation and interpretation, it has concerned itself more with the transaction between text and reader in the same way that it has always attended to the transaction between author and text. Literary criticism has been highly active, then, in the study of the subjective paradigm of which Bleich speaks.

One of the objections raised against reader-response criticism has been that it precludes the possibility of a definitive reading, that is, any one true and final interpretation. It is precisely this point, however, that is its strength and essence, because no method of analysis can reduce a literary text to a single meaning. The very nature of the literary work defies this sort of reduction. Furthermore, every text, as it is read, becomes intimately bound to the personality and to the environment of the reader. Equally, it is bound to the personality and environment of the author, making the study of a writer's biography and history important in the understanding of a work. Readers in the twentieth century, however, cannot know the psyche of a nineteenth-century author. We have only history (both of the writer and of the time), the text, and ourselves with which to work. Literary meaning cannot be separated from the reader, just as the meaning and definition of the object cannot be separated from the observer. Indeed, the two are closely linked through the act of observation, or, in the case of literature, through the act of reading. Despite the small measure of disorder the diversity of subjective response admits into the body of criticism, attention to that response allows us to consider many valid interpretations without violating the integrity of the text itself. Even more importantly, such attention reveals to us numerous subtleties within a text that have heretofore gone unnoticed. It permits us to combine our roles of reader and critic, at once admitting our personal involvement in the text and making use of the many clear, precise, and scientific tools with which we analyze the text, ourselves, and the transaction between the two.[15] Reception theory has engendered not only interesting textual analyses but also compelling studies of aesthetic perception and the process of reading.

The approach used in this study is based on current reception theory.[16] I treat the literary text as a highly dynamic entity, defining it as the vehicle of meaning, the axis of communication between author and reader, the creative field in which meaning is generated through the cooperative efforts of these two. A work can then be seen, I believe, in its fullest dimensions, not as a blank screen upon which are projected the fantasies of the reader, but as a skillfully constructed ensemble of story, language, and image that awaits its reader's dramatic fulfillment. Moreover, with each reading of a masterpiece, we evolve new levels of interpretation, progressively uncovering new depths and creating new meaning within. A significant work is constructed so as to allow and to guide our creativity. Balzac's *Comédie humaine* is a combination of a great many such works and is thus, because of its breadth and unity, a particularly rich object of study. The intricacy of Balzac's work and the author's clear concern in his texts for the reader's creative activity render our involvement in *La Comédie humaine* both complex and essential. At the same time, however, his conception of the whole and his sophisticated use of stylistic techniques define and control our participation in and contribution to the work.

As critical interest in reader response has grown throughout the twentieth century, the definition of the nature of the literary work and its relation to the reader as well as the understanding of how literary meaning is produced have changed.

In 1929, I. A. Richards greatly altered the perspective of both criticism and teaching with the publication of *Practical Criticism*. Clearly, Richards believed in the objective text and in the possibility of arriving at a definitive interpretation. But his analysis of students' responses to some poems was one of the first efforts of a critic to confront the reader's subjectivity. Richards did not hesitate to admit that the source of diversity in reader response lay deep in the unconscious. He denied, however, the value of any probing therein and sought only to correct errors in reading.[17]

In 1954, W. K. Wimsatt, Jr., and Monroe C. Beardsley decried what they called "The Affective Fallacy," a confusion between the poem and its results.[18] For them the meaning of a literary work was quite separate from its effect on the reader, and subjectivity in criticism led only to impressionism and relativism.

In 1957, *Fiction and the Unconscious*, by Simon Lesser, a strict follower of Freud, was published.[19] Indeed, Lesser initiated the serious use of psychoanalytic principles in the study of literature. He believed that literature "represents an attempt to augment the meager satisfactions offered by experience through the creation of a more harmonious world to which one can repair, however briefly, for refuge, solace and pleasure."[20] In Lesser's analysis, the material of fiction is psychic conflict that arouses tension in the reader and then relieves it; he thus defined the literary work in terms of the experience it provokes. Reading, in Lesser's terms, is a source of satisfaction for the psyche as defined by Freud. Fully ten years after his book appeared, the active study of reader response began.

The first significant book to build upon Lesser's study was *The Dynamics of Literary Response* by Norman N. Holland, which proposed the model of literature as transformation of the basic psychic issues or as the transformation of a central fantasy to be discovered and interpreted by the reader.[21] In *5 Readers Reading,* Holland analyzed not only the vastly different responses of five students of literature to Faulkner's "A Rose for Emily" but also the very process of reading that evolves and permits such diversity of response.[22] He altered his original model of literature in demonstrating that a transformation can take place only in the reader—not in the text. It is in the transaction or convergence between text and reader, he argued, that the transformation of psychic issues is to be found. The principles of that transformation are proposed in four clearly defined steps in the process of reading.

Equally significant, although more philosophically oriented, are the writings of David Bleich.[23] For Bleich, no literary meaning exists independent of that which the subjective reader creates. All critical interpretation is subjective, despite the obvious and quite natural attempt on the reader's part to objectify response. In "The Subjective Character of Critical Interpretation," Bleich claimed,

> the truth about something that requires an audience to gain reality is a different sort of thing than the truth about something that does not. The truth about the Newtonian Bible is different from the truth about the Newtonian apple. The truth of the Bible requires the faith of the reader; the truth of the acceleration of gravity does not. The truth about literature has no meaning independent of the truth about the reader.[24]

Other critics have considered the question of the reader in a significantly different manner. In "The Writer's Audience is Always a Fiction," Walter J. Ong suggested that every writer fictionalizes an audience, casts it in a specific role, and calls upon it to assume that role.[25] He further analyzed the question of communication between author and reader through the text by suggesting that the audience also must fictionalize itself and accept the role imposed on it by the author. Ong did not in this article test his theory by examining a work in order to show through what means the text communicates to its readers the role that the author has fictionalized for them or in what ways the readers play out the role that they see for themselves within the text.

In *The Implied Reader*,[26] Wolfgang Iser concentrated not upon the reader but upon the text, in order to lay the foundation for a theory about the nature of literary effects and reader reactions, which he put forth in *The Act of Reading: A Theory of Aesthetic Response*.[27] Iser's thesis is that the text contains a prestructured potential meaning that is actualized by the reader through the process of reading, which is itself a highly dynamic activity. Reading is the convergence of the text and the reader's imagination, the point at which meaning appears, not in one or the other but in the combination of the two. This approach permits Iser to study not only the contribution of an objective text but also the process by which the reader reads, in order to understand the reasons behind interpretations. The convergence of text and reader is what Iser refers to as the text's "virtual dimension."[28] This, of course, is the very transaction of which Holland spoke.

Combining approaches that concentrate on the text with those that focus on the reading process is essential to our understanding of the literary work as a form of communication: "Le texte de fiction doit être considéré avant tout comme une communication et l'acte de lecture, comme une relation dialogique"[29] ("The fictional text must be considered before all else as communication and reading as a dialogue"). To consider the text as squarely placed between the author and the reader permits us to see it as a transformation in and of itself, but also as existing in a constant state of transformation because it is a dynamic structure upon which interpretations are continually (or with each reading) made. The transformations worked through the literary text by author and reader alike are of stories themselves, of psychic conflicts and constructs, of the individual perception of social reality, and even of history.

In this study, I will pay primary attention to textual analysis, in order to delineate and refine an understanding of the processes through which meaning is produced in Balzac's work. It is, of course, within the text that the author has laid the plan for his reader, and it is on the work that we focus in our inevitable subjective interpretation and elaboration of the narration.

The diversity of interpretation given to a single literary text testifies to an author's ability to exert only partial control over the reception of his or her work, however. "Meaning is the referential totality which is implied by the aspects contained in the text and which must be assembled in the course of reading."[30] This process of assembly is our function as readers and our source of pleasure within the act of reading. A narrative must be constructed so as to take into account the many active readers who will interpret the fictional material in ways proper to their own experience. Thus, strategies that operate on many levels at once for the accommodation and manipulation of the active participant in the literary process are essential to narration. It is not hard to imagine that Balzac, an author who created an environment of social determinism for his characters, created one as well for his readers. I hope to demonstrate that Balzac did indeed create for us a deterministic setting, a social milieu of the reading that guides our thought and shapes our response, thus defining for us the *basis* of our interpretation.

The reading process itself, then, must be seen in the larger context of communication, of a special dual relationship, of a pact between author and reader. It is, of course, more than a simple decoding of the complexities built into the text. Inevitably, reading calls upon the past and present experience of the reader and plays upon the chaotic material of the unconscious. An individual reading is a rich blend of the cognitive and the sensuous; although we must respond cognitively to the words of the text, we are drawn in as well by its sensuousness, by rhythm, rhyme, and sound. We react both emotionally and intellectually to all levels of the narration, and at times we even respond physically. Grasped cognitively by the reader and elaborated subjectively, the text expands endlessly. The potential for this enormous expansion is present at all times within the text as the cognitive, that is, literal, material of the work assumes its broader dimensions through the reading process. Were the emotional and the sensuous carefully incorporated in the text itself, we would all receive approximately the same meaning, relative to the degree of our perspicacity, which, of course, we do not. In other types of communication, conversation for example, the listener has the advantage (if it is indeed an advantage) of such aids as voice, gesture, attitude, or facial expression to guide the interpretation. In literature, however, the depths of meaning that the work assumes and the reactions that it evokes depend on the reader's participation, which the author must subtly control through the text itself.[31]

Manipulating, shaping, and reshaping of the text are the activities of author and reader alike. The literary work is approached from both poles of the axis of communication. Iser has articulated the task of the reader vis-à-vis the text.

> Each sentence correlate contains what one might call a hollow section, which looks forward to the next correlate, and a retrospective section, which answers the expectations of the preceding sentence (now a part of the remembered background). Thus every moment of reading is a dialectic of protension and retension, conveying a future horizon yet to be occupied, along with a past (and continually fading) horizon already filled; the wandering viewpoint carves its passage through both at the same time and leaves them to merge together in its wake. There is no escaping this process, for . . . the text cannot at any one moment be grasped as a whole. . . . the aesthetic object is constantly being structured and restructured.[32]

It is revealing to consider the text in this light, especially realizing that it is just this sort of activity that the author must anticipate when designing the narration.

It is significant within this context to ask why we enter into the relationship required by the reading of imaginative literature. The many answers to the question explain some of the expectations that we bring to a work. The most fundamental and, one would hope, the most pervasive answer is that we read for the sheer pleasure of it. Pleasure, like so much else that touches us, is linked to our psyche and orientation, and pleasure, it can be argued, is linked to our need and desire for mastery.

In *Beyond the Pleasure Principle*, Freud speculated that play and the active representation by children of real-life situations are means by which they gain mastery of those parts of their lives over which they have little control.[33] In another essay, he further proposed that the adult activities of creative imagining and daydreaming are simply continuations of that play and serve a similar purpose.[34] If writing, which is the imposition of order and meaning upon the unordered, is a form of mastery, which it clearly is, then we can justly suppose that reading is also an activity that seeks to gain control and mastery, for it too imposes order and meaning. This is, of course, a widely held view of reading. But the activity of the reader is further similar to writing in the process by which meaning is produced. Reading is the restructuring of material already structured into meaning. We achieve an interpretation through our imaginative reconstruction of the author's written structure in the way that our own psychic orientation wishes and allows. If this model of a mental process is valid, then reading is an activity closely tied to the pleasure principle, which Freud defined as "a tendency . . . to free the mental apparatus entirely from excitation or to keep the amount of excitation in it constant or to keep it as low as possible."[35] The excitation of which Freud speaks here is a psychic excitation that is a source of "unpleasure," the state that the psychic apparatus seeks at most times to avoid. Reading is an activity clearly in the service of the pleasure principle. We simply do not (unless specifically required to do so by some outside force) read works that arouse great conflict and then do not resolve it. It is not difficult to imagine, for example, that scene after scene of bodily violence in a story might arouse more conflict and discomfort than a reader could bear. Freud believed that at the heart of every literary text there was a "raw issue," a central or focal conflict, and that the genius of the great writer was to disguise it in so acceptable a form that it would be recognized by readers without arousing in them a need to defend against it. In Freud's terms, the inferior work is one that offers its audience either too little or too much conflict. In either case, the reader would put the book aside. Thus, if violence were unacceptable to the given reader's psyche, that reader would defend against it by exercising the ultimate control, closing the book. This definition of an artistic creation is highly reductive, and it was written to serve Freud's own theories. It is, nevertheless, an interesting perspective from which to view literature, especially when we consider a reader's expectations.

Although it may seem obvious that a reader does not read that which arouses too much conflict, it is an important observation. That we can reject a text at any moment in our reading allows us to involve ourselves in it safely. The distance that we enjoy from a text, the constant knowledge that it is only a story, allows us a freedom we do not enjoy in our daily intercourse. Sensing that reading is a safe activity and that we are ultimately in control, we can allow such internal conflicts to be aroused as would ordinarily be unacceptable to us. Because we are not threatened by any real consequences, we can take psychic risks that would, in our other activities, be too conflictive. Indeed, we often enjoy literature that is a good deal more adventuresome than our lives, because reading allows us control, mastery, and resolution of conflict.

However, it is not only for the danger and the adventure that we enjoy reading. We also read with some interest that which is quite familiar to us. Balzac fully recognized and exploited the interest that we have in ourselves and our own milieu. But this interest is also psychically based. It is far more than simply seeing how a common situation may be handled within a fictional setting. It is permitting familiar tensions to well up once again, but without any real threat and with assurance of resolution. Although reading can be an escape from the daily routine, it can also be an escape into the self, without the dangerous consequences that we know and defend ourselves against daily. We would seem then to answer the question "Why do we read?" by saying that we read in part for therapeutic gains that result from communication at a psychic level. An author, then, must within the narration accommodate our expectations of involvement, escape from and into self, conflict and its resolution, and manipulation, yet disguise that control sufficiently so as to allow us our creativity.

Acknowledging that we read not only for the objective and conscious reasons we would all offer in response to the question of why one reads but also for far deeper, highly subjective, and probably unconscious reasons as well, leads us to question the process of reading itself and to pose yet another question, "How do we read?"

Wayne C. Booth was the first to speak of the "mock reader," a term he coined in discussing his own "inability or refusal to take on the characteristics [Lawrence] requires of his 'mock reader.' "[36] Other writers since Booth have used other names for this reader who is a mental (conscious or unconscious) construct of the author. Gérard Genette named him the "narrataire,"[37] a term referring to a fictional recipient of the text who can be either intratextual or extratextual. The narrataire becomes a construct of the text (if only during its writing) by playing the role of the reader, whether in the author's mind or in the text itself. When this construct truly plays a part in a story, that is, becomes an actual character, the reader cannot help but identify with the role of recipient, if not with the actual character. The transaction between reader and mock reader differs with each work and with each reader. In general, we attempt to reduce the distance between the actual self and the fictional self, an activity in part controlled by the text itself. Assuming the role of the mock reader, accepting the role imposed on us (be it that of confidant, eavesdropper, removed audience, or simple spectator) is a form of role playing, and aside from being among the great pleasures of reading, it is one of the primary maneuvers that reading requires. As Walter J. Ong has pointed out,

> Readers over the ages have had to learn this game of literacy, how to conform themselves to the projections of the writers they read, or at least how to operate in terms of these projections. They have to know how to play the game of being a member of an audience that "really" does not exist. And they have to adjust when the rules change, even though no rules thus far have ever been published and even though the changes in the unpublished rules are themselves for the most part only implied.[38]

The reader's entry into the narration is, then, the actual taking on of the role of reader; it is becoming a member of an audience. It is more than the willing suspension of disbelief of which Coleridge spoke, although that is certainly part of it. By taking on the role of reader, we assume a position in relation to the work, that of recipient, actualizer, and recreator. We make an effort to become the narrataire within the text, and we act as if we were—that is, we have a sense of being addressed when we read. Our goal is to break down the barrier between ourselves and the text in order to internalize the narration. Only upon internalization can fiction be objectified, and only then can it be manipulated subjectively.

Norman N. Holland has described in considerable detail this process of internalization and manipulation, acknowledging thereby the individual creativity of the reader. As he states in his preface to 5 Readers Reading, literary response involves "a transformation by means of forms acting like defenses, of drives, impulses, and fantasies back and forth from the most primitive strata of psychic life to the highest."[39] He delineates four principles of literary experience that chronologically outline the four stages of reading necessary to effect internalization of the message. According to Holland, we first test a text to see that it will gratify us in a psychically satisfactory fashion. We seek, he states, defenses and adaptations that are acceptable, if not similar to our own. In these stages, we treat the fictional narrative as an outside reality. If, however, it passes our psychic tests of fire, we allow it to be internalized; we become fully engaged in the reading. In the next phase, we use the text and our reading of it to build wish-fulfilling fantasies consistent with our psychic life. Finally, we will receive, shape, and interpret the text in a way characteristic of all our subjective activity. Having accepted the text, we master it along with our own unconscious conflicts.

The transaction between text and reader, however, is not dominated consistently by the reader, whose activity is in constant tension with the text that exerts its influence and control. Just as the reading process is essential to actualization of the text, so too the guidance of the strategies within the text is essential to the reading process. As Iser has clearly established, literary meaning remains always virtual, wholly present neither in the reality of the text nor in the disposition of the reader. The dynamic nature of the text itself is linked to this virtuality. We become involved in movement within the text and within ourselves, linking past, present, and future of the reading, building intratextual memories and expectations, associating and combining elements of the text, and hypothetically completing it. The truly dynamic and challenging text is the one that resists our efforts to maintain equilibrium, that keeps us off balance by continually frustrating our expectations and destroying our illusions, thus forcing us into an ever more active reading. "In seeking the balance we inevitably have to start out with certain expectations, the shattering of which is integral to the esthetic experience."[40] But this free movement within the text permits us to unify it and to see relationships that are significant in and of themselves. If the aesthetic pleasure of reading depends in part on this dynamic process within the context of an individual story or novel, how much greater must be the pleasure for the reader of *La Comédie humaine,* in which each work is related to a network of others and in which we perform our operations intertextually as well as intratextually.

The philosophical stance of reception theorists is significant for the purposes of this study. They stress the dynamism of the transaction effected through the reading process and the centrality of manipulation of the text by author and reader alike. They acknowledge the goal of internalization and objectification that is part of our response to the text, and they recognize the importance of our psychic, historical, and cultural orientation. What is not stressed in their work, however, although it is certainly implied, is the relationship of the influence that the work exerts to the design of the author. The narrative strategies constituting that design precede and shape our reading, and an understanding of how they operate in Balzac's writing will permit us to grasp more fully the meaning of his work, his mastery of his craft, and our continued pleasure and fascination with his fictional world. It will permit us to illuminate the creative process by which the fictional universe of *La Comédie humaine* is shaped.

II

THE CREATION OF THE REFERENT:
METAPHOR AS A MEANS OF CONTROL

> But if we are absorbed into an image, we are
> no longer present in a reality—instead we
> are experiencing what can only be described
> as an irrealization, in the sense that we
> are preoccupied with something that takes
> us out of our own given reality.
>
> Iser, *The Act of Reading*

In a study of controls structured within the text to shape the reader's response, a central focus of concern must be the metaphor. By its very nature, the metaphor implies a communicative act between author and reader, for it requires the creative vision of the author as well as the imagination of the reader for its meaning to be realized. As "une figure par laquelle on transporte, pour ainsi dire, la signification propre d'un mot à une autre signification qui ne lui convient qu'en vertu d'une comparaison qui est dans l'esprit"[1] ("a figure by which one transfers, so to speak, the proper meaning of a word to another meaning that only fits it by virtue of an imaginative comparison"), metaphor is clearly subject to the interpretation of its recipient and therefore never fixed in its meaning. Much of the literary value of the metaphor comes from the special relationship that it establishes with the reader. Because even the simplest of metaphors is capable of engendering a multiplicity of connotations, even more than nonfigured language, it requires and invites the hermeneutic act of the reader. But of particular interest in the Balzacian metaphor to be studied here are the ways in which the author has structured the image so that he controls our interpretation while allowing us an inevitable creative rendering of it.

As an image itself and as a narrative and structural element, the metaphor is a concentration of implications, suggestions, and energies. It draws us into the narration, emotionally as well as intellectually, as we work to grasp the image, develop it, and apply it to the various levels of the unfolding narrative. The metaphor is a textual magnet capable of drawing many narrative levels into it, focusing the heightened attention of the reader, and elevating the narration and the act of reading to a poetic plane. Ultimately, then, it must be carefully constructed into the narration, its appearance prepared, and its effect calculated.

In the skillful use of metaphor, authors have a special vehicle for the evocation of their visions of reality. The metaphor seizes our attention, forces us to focus on a new and different meaning, on a level of poetic implication that the strangeness of the metaphor invites us to elaborate. From the moment we perceive it within a narration, we work to interpret the juxtaposition of two terms or the analogy upon which the metaphor is based, moving immediately beyond the denotative level of language to the connotative. Because of an incompatibility between the terms of the metaphor on the denotative level, we are forced to focus on an abstraction and to develop it. "L 'incompatibilité sémantique joue le rôle d'un signal qui invite le destinataire à sélectionner parmi les éléments de signification constitutifs du lexème ceux qui ne sont pas incompatibles avec le contexte"[2] ("Semantic incompatibility functions as a signal to the receiver to select from among the elements of meaning that constitute the lexeme [morpheme] those that are not incompatible with the context"). Intrinsic, then, within the metaphor and the process of its successful actualization is a mechanism by which an author can shape our perception of a fictional reality. Equally important to the creation of meaning from the image, however, are the imagination and experience of the reader. Despite careful construction within the narration (carried to the extreme in the Balzacian text to be studied), a metaphor allows the author relatively little control over its reception, since its requisite ambiguity, tension, and difficulty, to use Umberto Eco's terms,[3] launch the reader instantly into a flight of imagination and abstraction. What control over that involvement the author does exert must be structured into the image itself. The reader's function within the metaphor that I analyze below is particularly clear and the process by which we uncover and create the links between the two terms of the metaphor unusually visible.[4] When we as readers are successfully engaged in the textual strategy that metaphor implies, a particularly vivid illusion of reality results. Whether subtle or heavy-handed, the metaphor is one of the most intriguing of textual strategies in its relationship to the reader.

Given the large scheme that Balzac envisioned within *La Comédie humaine*, the essence of social reality that he hoped to portray, and the consciousness of craft that his writing manifests, the metaphor should hold a central position in his work. Indeed, the importance of metaphoric expression within *La Comédie humaine* has been studied by Lucienne Frappier-Mazur.[5] Her work treats in splendid depth not only theory but also several specific metaphors (games, social situations, and aggression, to name but three) that function on the broad scale of Balzac's enormous work. In this study, however, I am looking at metaphor solely as a means by which Balzac was able to control reader response while accommodating and engaging the active reader. I have chosen a single metaphor, that of the "symphonie en ut mineur de Beethoven" (the Fifth Symphony), found in *Histoire de la grandeur et de la décadence de César Birotteau*. Concentration upon this text permits me to consider in some detail the processes of creating the image as well as the way in which it functions vis-à-vis the reader. Thus, the image of the symphony is of particular interest because it is marked (some would say marred) by the author's concern for its reception. Balzac's efforts to control our interpretation and understanding of the relationship of the symphony to his main character are clearly visible within the narration itself. It is not even upon the image, then, that I will concentrate, but upon the creative processes of author and reader that actualize it, especially those of the former. I selected this image not for its success as an image (although I find it most successful) but for all that it reveals to us about the functioning of metaphor within Balzac's writing. René Guise, in his introduction to the 1977 Pléïade edition of *César Birotteau*, pointed out that the novel contains some weaknesses, contradictions, and mixed messages (6:3–34). Despite the weaknesses that he so accurately delineates, and despite the fact that the passages on the Beethoven symphony were added to the novel at a later date,[6] development of the symphony as a metaphor within the text itself is extremely tight. Many other metaphors within Balzac's work are not so demonstrative in establishing a communication between author and reader, in facilitating the creation of a fictional reality, or even in serving as commentary upon the artistic endeavors of reading and writing. A consideration of this particular text, then, permits us to view the metaphor as a concentration of creative energies from the two poles of the axis of communication and to see as well the means by which Balzac has tied the poetic image to a narrative structure, to themes, and to description in order to shape our reading. By choosing this highly developed and perhaps obvious metaphor, I hope to show a complicated and textually contained metaphoric process by which Balzac shaped and guided reader response to his protagonist and to his narration.

The challenge to which this metaphor responds is one of the simultaneous exploration and portrayal of psychic depths, of the reality we call the unconscious. In his *Notes philosophiques*,[7] Balzac recorded a desire to find adequate language, "un langage de signes conventionnels" ("a language of conventional signs") that would "empêcher les erreurs de s'y glisser" ("prevent errors from creeping in") and by its functioning would also have the potential "d'atteindre les choses les plus inconnues et de déchirer les derniers voiles de la nature" ("to reach the most unknown things and to tear away the last veils of nature"). Although in this particular entry Balzac was discussing the substitution of ordinary language for that of metaphysics, his quest for an adequate means of expression is significant. The question of language implies Balzac's concern not only for his craft but also for the reception of his fiction. Metaphor as a generative form of language, expanding and intensifying with its reception and development, goes beyond the simple devices of mimetic language. In order to evoke the complex psychological condition of César, Balzac exploited the equally complex strategy of the metaphor. To complicate the relationship further, he chose for his metaphor the highly subjective world of music. René Guise spoke of the padding with which Balzac filled *César Birotteau* and of the role it plays in portraying the milieu of the period. According to Guise, the contemporary response to the work was cool—precisely because of its realistic treatment of the Parisian financial world that readers preferred to ignore. But the metaphor of the symphony enabled Balzac to explore deeper mysteries than those of nineteenth-century financial institutions and to represent, not through mimetic skills but through poetic evocation, the effect of social rise and fall upon the mental state of the protagonist. The addition of the symphony passages to this novel was most fortunate, resulting in the powerful metaphor that develops through them and in the role that they play in uniting author and reader in a process of characterization. Rather than the incorporation of a metaphor into the text, these passages offer us a metaphor in the making, a gradual creation of resemblances between the two quite separate worlds, and finally, the systematic substitution of one for the other. The image of the Beethoven symphony in *César Birotteau* becomes the articulation of that which cannot be articulated but by poetic language. While its careful construction within the text does not make it the most "rewarding" of metaphors (in Eco's terms), it is, nonetheless, one that demonstrates most clearly the nature of the convergence of author, text, and reader that metaphor fosters.

The choice of Beethoven's Fifth Symphony for metaphor in *César Birotteau* was deliberate. It is likely that the author heard a performance of it conducted by F. A. Habeneck in May of 1834.[8] In 1837, when he probably heard the Fifth Symphony again, he was reminded of an evening with Mme Hanska when together they heard a portion of the *Symphonie pastorale*. We find his impression of Beethoven's music in a letter to her dated

7 November 1837, written shortly before the description that we find in *César Birotteau*; much of the language used and most certainly the tone of the letter are identical to that which he incorporated into the text.

> Il y a dans cet homme [Beethoven] une puissance divine. Dans son *finale*, il semble qu'un enchanteur vous enlève dans un monde merveilleux, au milieu des plus beaux palais qui réunissent les merveilles de tous les arts et là, à son commandement, des portes, semblables à celles du Baptistère, tournent sur leurs gonds et vous laissent apercevoir des beautés d'un genre inconnu, les fées de la fantaisie, ce sont des créatures qui voltigent avec les beautés de la femme et les ailes diaprées de l'ange, et vous êtes inondé de l'air supérieur, de cet air qui, selon Swedenborg, chante et répand des parfums, qui a la couleur et le sentiment et qui afflue et qui vous béatifie.[9]

> (There is a divine power in this man [Beethoven]. In his finale, it is as if a magician raises you up to a marvelous world among the most beautiful palaces that bring together the miracles of all the arts. And there, at his order, doors, like those of the baptistry, turn on their hinges, permitting you to know unheard of beauties. Fantastic fairies hover with female beauty and the speckled wings of the angel. You are bathed in this refined air, in this air that, according to Swedenborg, sings and pours perfumes of color and of feeling that rush and that sanctify you.)

To understand the symphony passages in *César Birotteau*, we must realize that Balzac has articulated in the novel his personal experience as recipient, his subjective response to a specific portion and performance of Beethoven's music. The relationship between the author's response to the music and the response he attempted to evoke from the reading public will become clear within the narration itself.

Beyond basing his image upon a personal aesthetic experience, Balzac chose to make the image that of a performance rather than of an object and thereby built on something fundamentally dynamic and untranslatable by the word. Thus, in order to represent that which cannot be put into words, the psychological state of a fictional character, Balzac used a dynamic literary technique, the metaphor, and, further, chose as one pole of the metaphor that which cannot itself be translated by the word, the performance of the finale of the Beethoven symphony. At both poles of the developing metaphor, Balzac was working in a relationship other than that of word-to-thing. Metaphor itself is not, of course, based upon such a relationship either. The complex process by which the symphony comes to represent within *César Birotteau* the psychological state of the character is a process of pure evocation of experience beyond language, the recreation within the reader of an experience of the author and the controlled application of that experience to the narrative. The relationship between Balzac and a performance of the symphony is articulated in such a way that a new relationship develops between the articulation and the reader. From that latter relationship grows a third, between the reader's experience of the passage and interpretation of César. Martin Kanes maintained that in Balzac's work, "Musicality in language and music as language are therefore vehicles of human expression, capable of conveying meaning that does not duplicate the meaning embodied in the referentiality of words."[10] I would go even further: in this particular passage the metaphor of music is meaning in a purely potential state; the metaphor can be actualized only to the degree that it is able to evoke an experience in the reader and to shape that reader's translation of experience into meaning.

Of course, it is not the symphony we encounter through our reading, but words. Balzac did not depend on readers' familiarity with the actual symphony (over which he would have had no control), but sought to create with us a new experience, offering us within the text not only the signifier but also the signified. Any actual performance of the symphony—even one that Balzac himself experienced—is insignificant, for he created a new referent for his image, a new finale for the "symphonie en ut mineur." Had Balzac relied upon some collective experience of the symphony, he would have surrendered control over the reception of the image and its interpretation. Instead, Balzac provided the field for a constantly renewable experience through reading, over which his efforts continue to exert a great deal of control. Balzac directed those efforts not to César or even to the narrative at hand but to his readers and their reception of the metaphor. It is a circuitous route by which to shape our grasp of the character, yet it is one more certain than familiarity with the symphony to allow the author control and the reader subjective and creative response.

There are but two passages within *César Birotteau* that involve the symphony. Significantly, each portion of the novel ends with one of these passages. Only in its second appearance however, does it function fully as a metaphor and then only because of the careful elaboration of the first passage. The creation of the signified, or fictional, referent is effected through the first passage and eliminates dependence on the world outside the novel. Its creation insists on the autonomous nature of the image, on the intrinsic nonreferentiality of the language used to develop it, and on the symphony as a poetic and linguistic element within the text. Furthermore, the autonomy of the image encloses us as readers within the narrative where, indeed, our response is more easily controlled. According to Paul Ricoeur, the terms of the metaphor are often overdetermined.[11] In this case, however, a good part of the process of that determination is visible within the text and becomes the means by which we are controlled. In the first appearance of the symphony, we encounter the formation of the image. We find the development of the "systèmes d'implications spécialement construits" ("specially constructed systems of implications") at the heart of the metaphor.[12] Surely, for some this rather obvious determination within the text itself weakens the strength of the metaphor by reducing the possibility of free and spontaneous reader response by rendering the whole process less subtle. If indeed the goal of the image making is to unleash the reader's creativity, then this development is not a happy one. But Balzac's goal seems to have been to ease us into an experience, to engage us in this representation on the affective level. The author's careful elaboration reduces our own such work, freeing us, at least at this juncture, to experience the passage more on an affective than on an intellectual level. In the second appearance of the symphony, our role combines the intellectual with the affective and is far more exacting in the demands it makes. But the careful elaboration of the first part serves to restrict the image of the symphony in such a way that its unity is internal to the text and its nature essentially aesthetic (as opposed to referential). Its communicative powers are not then "scientific or referentially descriptive" but poetic.[13]

The image of the symphony can barely be separated in this novel from the enormously detailed description of the ball that celebrates César's social advancement. The scene of the ball is prepared for from the opening pages of the novel so that it becomes the long-awaited event for character and reader alike. The metaphor will represent the harmony and joy of the character at the ball with all that it represents. The ball itself then is woven into the fabric of the narration at every level. Thus, the careful preparation for both the ball and the metaphor permits the latter to become the convergence point of all levels of the text. That preparation is far too lengthy to illustrate here, but a few examples of the connection of the ball to various levels of the story will be useful. As it is first announced, it is tied to the caricature of César and simultaneously to his wife's fear over the expense of the ball. She awakens in the middle of the night from a nightmare in which she has seen herself impoverished and finds her husband taking measurements for the redecoration of the apartment. "Nous pouvons donner le bal" ("We can give the ball") is his announcement; her reply, "Donner un bal! nous? Foi d'honnête femme, tu rêves, mon cher ami" (6:41) ("Give a ball! us? On the word of an honest woman, you're dreaming, my dear friend"). In the first part of the novel, the caricature of César is drawn through a comical series of invitations to the grand ball. The attitude of the narrator toward the character, exhibited in part through sarcastic asides related to poor taste and foolish expenditure, is a superior one, and the reader is invited to share it and to view the ball as César's folly. At the same time, however, the ball celebrates the social rise of the character, his business success, his appointment to the Légion d'honneur, and his position in the government, adviser to the mayor. Analysis of the importance of the event is found throughout the first half of the novel as it is described from the outside (by jealous neighbors, the press, the architect who refurbishes the apartment) and from the inside (by César who is so proud and by Constance who is so fearful). Finally, because the reader is told early in the novel by the superior narrator that César's business speculations are doomed and that his demise has been carefully worked out by his enemy, the ball comes to represent the event that will ruin him financially. By the time we arrive at the ball itself, the narrator refers to it as "le fameux dimanche du dix-sept décembre" (6:162) ("that famous Sunday, the seventeenth of December"), and we know that it is both the grandest affair and the beginning of the end.

The narrator dwells long upon the ball's heaviness and its silliness, the excess of celebration, the sheer joy of César, the disgust of the few aristocrats in attendance. Throughout, the narrator maintains his superior and sarcastic tone. But momentum gathers as the dancing, the music, and the drinking all come together in a great swirl of activity. "Comme ils s'amusent! disait l'heureux Birotteau" (6:179) ("What fun they're having! said the happy Birotteau"). Finally, as if to jettison the momentum of the event to his own superior level and to represent the joy of César, the narrator offers us the analogy to the finale of the Fifth Symphony.

Dans l'oeuvre des huit symphonies de Beethoven, il est une fantaisie, grande comme un poème, qui domine le finale de la symphonie en *ut* mineur. Quand, après les lentes préparations du sublime magicien si bien compris par Habeneck, un geste du chef d'orchestre enthousiaste lève la riche toile de cette décoration, en appelant de son archet l'éblouissant motif vers lequel toutes les puissances musicales ont convergé, les poètes dont le coeur palpite alors comprendront que le bal de Birotteau produisait dans sa vie l'effet que produit sur leurs âmes ce fécond motif, auquel la symphonie en ut doit peut-être sa suprématie sur ses brillantes soeurs. Une fée radieuse s'élance en levant sa baguette. On entend le bruissement des rideaux de soie pourpre que des anges relèvent. Des portes d'or sculptées comme celles du baptistère florentin tournent sur leurs gonds de diamant. L'oeil s'abîme en des vues splendides, il embrasse une enfilade de palais merveilleux d'où glissent des êtres d'une nature supérieure. L'encens des prospérités fume, l'autel du bonheur flambe, un air parfumé circule! Des êtres au sourire divin, vêtus de tuniques blanches bordées de bleu, passent légèrement sous vos yeux en vous montrant des figures surhumaines de beauté, des formes d'une délicatesse infinie. Les amours voltigent en répandant les flammes de leurs torches! Vous vous sentez aimé, vous êtes heureux d'un bonheur que vous aspirez sans le comprendre en vous baignant dans les flots de cette harmonie qui ruisselle et verse à chacun l'ambroisie qu'il s'est choisie. Vous êtes atteint au coeur dans vos secrètes espérances qui se réalisent pour un moment. Après vous avoir promené dans les cieux, l'enchanteur, par la profonde et mystérieuse transition des basses, vous replonge dans le marais des réalités froides, pour vous en sortir quand il vous a donné soif de ses divines mélodies, et que votre âme crie: Encore! L'histoire psychique du point le plus brillant de ce beau finale est celle des émotions prodiguées par cette fête à Constance et à César. Collinet avait composé de son galoubet le finale de leur symphonie commerciale. (6:179–80)[14]

(Among the eight symphonies of Beethoven there is a theme, glorious as a poem, that dominates the finale of the Symphony in C Minor. When, after slow preparations by the sublime magician, so well understood by Habeneck, the enthusiastic leader of an orchestra raises the rich veil with a motion of his hand and calls forth the transcendent theme towards which the powers of music have all converged, poets whose hearts have throbbed at those sounds will understand how the ball of César Birotteau produced upon his simple being the same effect that this fecund harmony wrought in theirs—an effect to which the Symphony in C Minor owes its supremacy over its glorious sisters. A radiant spirit springs forward, lifting high her wand. You hear the rustle of the violet silken curtains that the angels raise. Sculptured golden doors, like those of the baptistry at Florence, turn on their diamond hinges. The eye is lost in splendid vistas: it takes in a long perspective of magnificent palaces where beings of a higher nature glide. The incense of all prosperities sends up its smoke, the altar of all joy flames, the perfumed air circulates! Beings with divine smiles, robed in white tunics bordered with blue, pass lightly before the eyes showing visages of supernatural beauty, shapes of an incomparable delicacy. The Loves hover in the air and spread the flames of their torches! You feel beloved: you are happy as you breathe in joy without understanding it, as you bathe in the waves of a harmony that flows for all, and pours out to all the ambrosia that each desires. You are held in the grasp of your secret hopes that are realized, for an instant, as you listen. When he has led you through the skies, the great magician, with a deep mysterious transition of the basses, flings you back into the marsh of cold reality, only to draw you forth once more when, thirsting for his divine melodies, your soul cries out, "Encore!" The psychical history of that rare moment in glorious finale of the C Minor Symphony is also that of the emotions excited by this fete in the souls of César and Constance. Collinet had sounded, with his flute, the last notes of their commercial symphony.)

In this passage, it is clearly announced to us that this is a high point within the symphony, within the life of César, and, we might assume, within the reading of the novel. The beauty of the symphony is established perhaps in an effort to communicate that the author's articulation of his own response to a performance is also a supreme moment within his narrative. The passage itself offers to us in miniature not only the evening of the ball, with its slow preparation that comprises much of the first half of the narrative, but also the rise and fall of César. Concentrated into the creation of the metaphor are several strains of the novel. The image of the symphony summarizes the first half of the narration and prefigures the second. Just as the finale is the point of convergence of musical strength ("toutes les puissances musicales ont convergé"), so too the ball will be the point of convergence of all the diverse narrative lines and the metaphor itself, the concentration of all important aspects of the narration, which will permit us to interpret the character of César. Furthermore, as the ball is the high point in the character's life, this passage is the high point of our reading. In creating for us a peak reading experience to parallel the experience of the character enjoying the ball, Balzac has encouraged a further convergence, between ourselves as readers and the text. The effort to induce an experience of harmony and joy for the reader fosters the reduction of distance between Balzac's narration and his reader and encourages the reader to internalize and personalize the narration in a way not previously carried out in *César Birotteau*. The first of the two symphony passages is directed, then, not only to the creation of the intratextual referent but specifically as well to the creation of a parallel experience for the reader. And that grand parallel is established through a set of smaller parallels that suggest to us the nature of our response.

The first of these parallels is a bit of flattery for the reader, suggesting that if we are "poets whose hearts have throbbed," we will understand the joy and harmony of César at the ball. As it flatters us for our possible sensitivity, it encourages us to respond poetically to the passage to come. As are poets to a performance of the symphony's finale, as is César to the celebration, so will be readers to the poetic passage in the making. We are prepared to accept Balzac's compliment because the narrator has placed us on a level equal to his own, that is, above César in matters of social standing and sensibility. We are consistently projected into the narration by the sarcasm of the narrator who shares his prejudices with us, as his penetrating eye informs us of the most secret thoughts of all the characters and as his panoramic view keeps us simultaneously informed of every segment of story line. The elevation of the image of the ball to the superior artistic level of the Beethoven symphony raises the narration to the level of the projected superior reader. The choice of the symphony, then, as a means of portraying an inferior reality is in accordance with the world of the fictional reader that the text implies. The symphony links the experience of César with that of the reader, the lowly world of the character with the elevated and artistic world of the reader, clearly demonstrating how the author can position us in relation to his text and shape our response and how he encourages us to accept the role of narrataire.

There is another significant parallel implied here, the projected experience of the reader prior to the passage with that of Balzac himself before hearing one of Beethoven's symphonies performed. Most readers would not know (although we might suspect it) that the description is in part an articulation of Balzac's own experience. But from Balzac's point of view, I maintain, this passage, because of its relationship to ideas found in Balzac's correspondence (cited above) and because of the strong projection of a fictional reader we find here, represents the novel's most intense moment of communication between the author and the actual reader. The passage is a break in the tone of the description of the ball, and, in fact, of the whole narration. It seems to bypass, or transcend, the narration itself, and very nearly the narrator, by a direct address to a fictional reader, by the use of elevated language, and by a highly poetic tone. The significance that we, or at least our fictional counterparts, are given in this passage so pointedly directed at us and at our response, then, subtly conditions our reception of the passage and lays the groundwork for the creation of the metaphor. Eventually, the metaphor will capture the essense of the entire narration and, more significantly, will mold our response to it.

Although the projection of the reader is relatively subtle, there is much within this passage that is not. In both its beginning and its end, Balzac's narrator dictates to us just how we should interpret the relationship of the finale to César's state of mind, intellectually manipulating the reader. But between the two intellectual attacks, there is another type of control exerted, as an attempt to manipulate the affective response is played off the more intellectual manipulation. The middle of the passage, where Balzac attempted to induce the peak reading experience, is its most significant section vis-à-vis the question of control of the reader.

In order to invoke an experience that the reader might interpret as parallel to the harmony and joy represented by the narration, Balzac has constructed a passage that becomes a call to the senses of the reader and an evocation of art and the mystical. Systematically it calls upon us to envision or to imagine, using three of our senses: hearing ("le bruissement des rideaux de soie pourpre" ["the rustle of violet silken curtains"], "les portes . . . tournent sur leurs gonds" ["doors . . . turn on their hinges"]; sight ("rideaux de soie pourpre" ["violet silken curtains"], "portes d'or sculptées" ["sculptured golden doors"], "gonds de diamant" ["diamond hinges"], "vues splendides" ["splendid vistas"], "une enfilade de palais merveilleux" ["a long perspective of magnificent palaces"], "tuniques blanches bordées de bleu" ["white tunics bordered with blue"], "figures surhumaines de beauté" ["beings with divine smiles"]); and touch ("vous baignant dans les flots de cette harmonie qui ruisselle et verse à chacun l'ambroisie qu'il s'est choisie" ["you bathe in the waves of a harmony that flows for all, and pours out to all the ambrosia that each desires"]). To underscore the experiential (as opposed to referential) nature of the passage even further, Balzac included movements that duplicate both the harmony and the intensity of the performance-ball: vibration, palpitation, convergence, elevation, rustling, pivoting, smoking, burning, circulating, soaring, floating, bathing, flowing, pouring. The sensuous movement invoked by

the passage glorifies César's experience, but more importantly, it captures readers in the movement of their own
reading. Balzac has thus offered us the realization of an experience, an invitation to play freely with the sensuousness of
the passage such that we may know the heights to which
César has soared. That free play of response is acknowledged
openly: "Vous êtes atteint au coeur dans vos secrètes espérances qui se réalisent pour un moment" ("You are held in the
grasp of your secret hopes that are realized, for an instant").
The acknowledgment and appreciation of a subjective response are immediately tempered, however, by a declaration
and a demonstration of the power of the aesthetic object:
"Après vous avoir promené dans les cieux, l'enchanteur . . .
vous replonge dans le marais des réalités froides, pour vous
en sortir quand il vous a donné soif de ses divines mélodies"
("When he has led you through the skies, the great magician
. . . flings you back into the marsh of cold reality only to
draw you forth once more when he has made you thirsty for his
divine melodies"). The entire symphony passage, an articulated response to a performance, becomes through our reading a performance in and of itself. Balzac must have hoped
that his performance would work upon us as the Beethoven
symphony had upon him, that we would experience firsthand
through the performance and the reception of this passage
the rise and fall of which the narration speaks; the convergence of story lines is effected in our performance-reading.
Like César in his financial dealings, we are plunged into
reality. For César, the plunge is into realization, fear, and
bankruptcy. For us, it is back into a less poetic narrative, back
to the superior and sarcastic tone that is the narrator's. The
distance between the fictional reader and the narration, reduced to almost nothing during the reading of this passage, is
reestablished. The peak reading experience, composed of sensuousness, movement, personalized address and response,
evokes an image of harmony, of excessive joy, of near-mystical
sensations.

It is not only the moment of highest intensity in our reading and the greatest moment for César, but it is also a moment at which the author's creative process, his efforts to

control the reception of the text, and the axis of communication between author and reader are most visible. The passage thus becomes an ellipsis or short cut in the channels of communication established within the text, as all levels converge momentarily to permit the reduction of distance between author and reader and between text and reader. From the reading of this passage, we carry not an intellectual image, but the experience of the "symphonie en ut mineur," and that experience permits the symphony to function as metaphor in its later appearance in the novel.

With the description of the ball, particularly within it, and with that of the symphony, the entire text of *César Birotteau* turns in a direction announced in the passage itself. Part 2, "César aux prises avec le malheur" ("César Battling with Misfortune"), leads us into what the narrator has called, in relation to the music, "le marais des réalités froides." Throughout the second half of the book, however, where we find the effects of César's bankruptcy, the symphony is not mentioned. The ball itself is referred to only occasionally and mostly in negative terms: "Maudit ball!" (6:187) ("Blasted ball!"); "Le diable seul a pu m'inspirer de donner ce bal" (6:192) ("The devil alone could have inspired me to give this ball"). It no longer symbolizes joy and honor, as it did in the first part, but César's destruction instead. The thread of the image of the symphony is not lost, however. We find it (albeit rarely) evoked in the structure and in the vocabulary of subtly placed passages. For example, "Birotteau dévoilait ainsi la profondeur de l'abîme où la main de du Tillet l'avait plongé, d'où elle le retirait, où elle pouvait le replonger" (6:218–19) ("In that way, Birotteau discovered the depth of the abyss into which du Tillet had flung him, from which he drew him out again, and into which he could thrust him once more"). Through the movement portrayed and the vocabulary used, this passage should remind attentive readers of their peak reading experience.

However, only at the end of the narration does the initially joyous image of the symphony return with metaphoric strength. Throughout the hard work of rehabilitation after bankruptcy, César, Constance, Césarine, and her fiancé Popinot have remembered the ball fondly, although silently. In the end, with César's financial rehabilitation in clear view, Popinot arranges for the family to sublet their old apartment, still intact as before, and he plans another ball to celebrate his wedding to Césarine. Except that it will be more modest, this ball is to duplicate the first one. It takes place on the day when César settles his debts and is reestablished in the financial world. He returns home from those extraordinary events to find the guests.

Lorsqu'en rentrant dans son ancienne maison il vit au bas de l'escalier, resté neuf, sa femme en robe de velours cerise, Césarine, le comte de Fontaine, le vicomte de Vandenesse, le baron de La Billardière, l'illustre Vauquelin, il se répandit sur ses yeux un léger voile, et son oncle Pillerault qui lui donnait le bras sentit un frissonnement intérieur.

"C'est trop, dit le philosophe à l'amoureux Anselme, il ne pourra jamais porter tout le vin que tu lui verses."

La joie était si vive dans tous les coeurs, que chacun attribua l'émotion de César et ses trébuchements à quelque ivresse bien naturelle, mais souvent mortelle. En se retrouvant chez lui, en revoyant son salon, ses convives, parmi lesquels étaient des femmes habillées pour le bal, tout à coup le mouvement héroïque du finale de la grande symphonie de Beethoven éclata dans sa tête et dans son coeur. Cette musique idéale rayonna, pétilla sur tous les modes, fit sonner ses clairons dans les méninges de cette cervelle fatiguée, pour laquelle ce devait être le grand finale. (6:311)

(He entered the house and saw at the foot of the staircase [still new as he had left it] his wife in her velvet gown, Césarine, the Comte de Fontaine, the Vicomte de Vandenesse, the Baron de la Billardière, the illustrious Vauquelin. A light film dimmed his eyes, and his uncle Pillerault, who held his arm, felt him shudder inwardly.

"It's too much," said the philosopher to the happy lover; "He can never handle all the wine you are pouring for him."

Joy was so strong in their hearts that each attributed César's emotion and his stumbling step to the natural intoxication of his feelings—natural, but often mortal. When he found himself once more in his own home, when he saw his salon, his guests, the women in their ball dresses, suddenly the heroic movement of the finale of the great symphony burst forth in his head and heart. Beethoven's ideal music echoed, vibrated, in many tones, sounding its clarions through the membranes of this weary brain, of which it was indeed the grand finale.)

The novel ends quickly, then, with César's death.

The reappearance of the symphony in this passage is determined, of course, by the story line, that is, by the reenactment of the event to which it was linked. Psychologically the character is once more at a peak, although a lower one than before. The harmony of the moment is more than he can bear. The excess is too great. Elements within the narration converge once again to precipitate the explosion of the symphony. In its second appearance, however, the symphony functions metaphorically, evoking once more its earlier, careful elaboration. Because of that development, the explosion of the symphony resonates with meaning for the reader. On the most superficial level, we are called upon to remember our experience of the reading and César's parallel experience, but we interpret the return of such a high pitch of excitement in view of the second half of the story. Through the metaphor, we quickly grasp César's new psychological state. Once again, it is that which was evoked in the first passage but this time fatally so; he has been devastated by recovery and dies.[15]

The metaphor of the symphony remains the articulation of a psychological and mental state, the poetic convergence of all levels of the narration. In the second part, we add to the rich image of harmony and intensity the connotation of destruction. The metaphor calls upon us to grasp the convergence of the many disparate levels of narration as it crystallizes and concentrates the numerous themes, incidents, and structures within. Like the "talismanic language" of which Kanes speaks, the symphony functions as metaphor here to "reflect major themes in the novels and help establish the conceptual points of view from which their events are seen."[16] Like the explosion of the symphony in César's head, the metaphor bursts upon the scene to recall our earlier peak reading experience and to invite us to reinterpret it. In contrast to that earlier passage, so tightly constructed to shape our experience of it, this one offers little to guide our interpretation. We are told that the music is "heroic" and "ideal," charged adjectives that surely suggest how to interpret the state of César Birotteau. But the strength of the image lies in its surprise appearance, in its strangeness, and in its power to evoke the poetry of an earlier reading experience. It thrusts us suddenly back into the domain of close communication with and reduced distance from the narration, subtly playing upon our emotions even as it encourages us to elaborate the image.

The metaphor by its very nature, and this one in particular by its associations and positioning, draws our attention to the text itself. With the reappearance of the symphony image, the narration closes in upon itself, forming an internal, cyclical structure. This is, of course, the structure of the narrative that follows the rise, fall, rise, and collapse of César. It is also the structure of the internal referent that Balzac has created, for the symphony too rises and falls. Even in its triumphant return at the end of the narration, the symphony signals the final destruction of the character. The cycle thus portrays a vision of society in which money and position are gained, lost, and regained in a constant social movement. But the internal structure upon which rests the functioning of this metaphor presents to us as well the model of the reader's activity. Each part brings our reading to a high point of intensity and experience. The metaphor itself forces us into a nonlinear reading as we necessarily return to the highest point in our experience. Having completed the novel, we then rework the narration along the lines of a new organization, which itself activates new levels of meaning tied to the generative circularity. Our grasp of this metaphor as metaphor (implying that we move in a cyclical, nonchronological direction) permits us to comprehend and to elaborate the image in its connotative multiplicity. Only a metaphor of such complexity, structured strategically within a text, could evoke the depth of meaning that Balzac designed this one to engender (truth of character, social reality, intensity of experience). In short, the metaphor of Beethoven's Fifth Symphony becomes the figurative expression of an entire fictional domain.

The circularity upon which the narration rests is also the basis for the functioning of the metaphor. As the creation of the signified in the first passage enclosed the reader within it, so too the metaphoric final appearance of the symphony encases the image itself within the narration. The metaphor is constructed upon a dynamic movement, but its referent as it appears in part 2 is only that which has been created between author and reader in the first part. The intratextual referentiality is what permits the image its freshness and renewability. According to Ricoeur, "L'énigme du discours métaphorique c'est, semble-t-il, qu'il 'invente' au double sens du mot: ce qu'il crée, il le découvre; et ce qu'il trouve, il l'invente"[17] ("The mystery of metaphoric discourse is, it seems, that it 'invents' in the double meaning of the word: that which it creates, it discovers; and that which it finds, it invents"). This definition invests the image with new meaning and makes of it a metaphor for the aesthetic experience as Balzac has portrayed it in his description of the symphony: cyclical, dynamic, constantly renewable—a performance in which the artist and the recipient converge. Making a metaphor of the symphony *within* the novel makes the latter a performance and an aesthetic object in its own right. That activity emphasizes, and perhaps exposes, the experiential and the creative aspects of our reading. The process of rapprochement, symbolized within and controlled through the metaphor, is that of the actual reader's internalization and manipulation of the aesthetic object.

The metaphor in *César Birotteau* is, then, an event. As an experience for the reader, it is carefully and visibly structured by Balzac. Through it we can actualize and elaborate much meaning within this narration. But this particular metaphor, perhaps more than others, demonstrates to us the means of control of which Balzac made use in order to guide us. It provides for us an unusual glimpse at the meeting of authorial control and reader response.

III

A MAP TO GUIDE US:
THE OPENING DESCRIPTION

Je ne cesserai de répéter que le vrai de la
nature ne peut pas être, ne sera jamais le
vrai de l'art; que, si l'art et la nature se
rencontrent exactement dans une oeuvre, c'est
que la nature, dont les hasards sont innom-
brables, est alors arrivée aux conditions de l'art.

(I shall never cease to repeat that the
truth of nature cannot be, and never will be,
the truth of art; and that if art and nature
meet perfectly in a work it is because
nature, whose changes are innumerable, has
arrived at the conditions of art.)

Balzac, "Lettres sur la littérature"

The popularity of Balzac's work, according to critic David
Bellos, reached a high point among nineteenth-century French
readers during the years 1856–1857, a high point as well of the
realist movement in French letters.[1] The realistic elements of
his work, long recognized for their contribution to the movement, were, of course, part of the artistic innovativeness of *La
Comédie humaine*, elements proper to the novel form that
the author helped to create. Although the lengthy descriptions with which Balzac opened many of his texts have been
both hailed and condemned for their realistic detail, this
particular narrative element, the opening description, is of
special interest within the context of my study. Indeed, it is
the basis of one textual strategy by which the author communicates to us the mode of reception required for complet-

ing his narration, and it is a narrative element about which Balzac has been very clear. In a passage to be examined here, he has indicated to us the role to be played by the description of the milieu of *La Recherche de l'absolu* as well as the way it should serve as intermediary between the narration and our interpretation of it. Although the formula Balzac established for the transaction between description and reader is rather simple, his descriptions direct our responses in subtle ways, demanding diversity and positioning us in relation to the text. Even his outright directives to the reader become part of a framework within which we are oriented toward and eased carefully into a mode of interpretation. Although the varying degrees of such manipulation are evident in many types of description within *La Comédie humaine*,[2] they are perhaps most clear and most easily analyzed in the descriptions that open narrations. For here we find the most attention paid to positioning readers and to communicating to them their primary function vis-à-vis the narration. Obviously, the opening description is the first contact with the reader, and, for that alone, its effect must be calculated.[3]

Many literary theoreticians consider the description an organizational point of the narration, a narrative element that offers the reader a textual introduction inscribed with meaning and directives. According to Philippe Hamon, "Lieu privilégié où s'organise (ou se détruit) la lisibilité de tout récit, la description se présente donc comme une sorte de 'réseau' sémantique à forte organization"[4] ("The description, a privileged place where the readability of every narration is organized [or destroyed], presents itself therefore as a sort of highly organized semantic 'network'"). Description offers an author a means by which to expand the text along a vertical axis, that is, in a direction different from that of the story line. Hamon called the description a paradigmatic expansion or prolongation that serves to deepen, to broaden, or to comment upon the horizontal plane of the text, the story line.[5]

The description (and it is particularly the case with the opening descriptions found in *La Comédie humaine*) functions narratively to position and to orient the readers. It offers us a perspective different from that which the narration or dialogue provides us. Roland Barthes has classified the description as "superior" language "dans la mesure apparemment paradoxale, où elle n'est justifiée par aucune finalité d'action ou de communication"[6] ("inasmuch, paradoxically, as it is not justified by any finality of action or communication").

Although there is in Balzac's texts a clear relationship between environment and character, or between environment and event, the description of that environment functions differently vis-à-vis the reader than does the narration. Opening descriptions in particular are designed to introduce us to the internal unity of the text and to pattern our reading and interpretation of it. In both function and structure they stand apart from the narration to which they are linked. Hamon claimed that description and narration are based on a different "linguistic consciousness," the latter dependent on a "logical foreseeability," in which concepts of correlation and difference are significant. For example, a door that opens will then close. Description, on the other hand, rests upon a "lexical foreseeability," in which concepts of inclusion and resemblance are most significant. For example, the term *rose* may engender others, *bouquet* and *petal*, *rosebush* and *rosary*, or it may suggest ideas of purity and virginity.[7] From these assertions, Hamon claimed, "toute description se présente donc comme un ensemble lexical métonymiquement homogène dont l'extension est liée au vocabulaire disponible de l'auteur, non au degré de complexité de la réalité elle-même"[8] ("every description presents itself therefore as a metonymically homogenous lexical whole, the extension of which is linked to the vocabulary available to the author and not to the degree of complexity of reality itself").

The referentiality of the description, then, is to itself and to the text into which we integrate it. Its referent is of its own creation. Thus, just as Balzac's descriptions of environment are linked to the development of character and story line, so too do they link the reader to the narration itself. As Patrick Imbert has pointed out, the Balzacian description does not denote but connotes reality. While it does have a "referential function," its "signifying function" is of far more importance.

The orientation of the Balzacian description is clearly not to the outside but "vers le roman composant un univers clos"[9] ("toward the novel composing a closed universe").

Like description in general, then, the opening descriptions within Balzac's works function on several levels, though principally to introduce the reading of the narration.[10] They become, as Gérard Genette has called the description in general, a "frontière intérieure du récit."[11] ("inner boundary of the narration").

Balzac's critical writing bears witness to his consciousness of the potential effect of the opening description on the reader. His discussion of James Fenimore Cooper's writing—he particularly admired Cooper as landscape artist—demonstrates his enthusiasm for the description as a powerful narrative element in its relationship to the reader and to the events of the story. In "Lettres sur la littérature," Balzac wrote of the dangers that Cooper described.

> Ces périls sont si bien liés aux accidents du terrain que vous examinez attentivement les rochers, les arbres, les chutes d'eau, les bateaux d'écorce, les buissons; vous vous incarnez à la contrée; elle passe en vous, ou vous passez en elle, on ne sait comment s'accomplit cette métamorphose due au génie; mais il vous est impossible de séparer le sol, la végétation, les eaux, leur étendue, leur configuration, des intérêts qui vous agitent. Enfin les personnages deviennent ce qu'ils sont réellement, peu de chose, dans cette grande scène que vous mesurez incessamment.[12]

> (The dangers are so allied to the lay of the land that you examine attentively the rocks, the trees, the rapids, the bark canoes, the bushes; you incarnate yourself in the country; it passes into you, or you into it, and you know not how this metamorphosis, the work of genius, has been accomplished; but you feel it impossible to separate the soil, the vegetation, the waters, their expanse, their configuration, from the interests that agitate you. The personages become what they really are, a small matter in this grand scene which your eye measures.)

Balzac was writing not only as an author concerned about relationships among narrative elements but as a reader as well, upon whom the description had a significant effect and whom we see here measuring and evaluating his own response. In Balzac's fiction, the descriptions of the urban landscape, the setting for many of his stories, reveal an effort to engage his readers much as Cooper did him. The opening descriptions were, in their structure and design, a means not only of capturing us in "cette grande scène" but also of constructing the framework for our interpretation of story, character, and narration itself.

The diversity with which Balzac opened his narrations is considerable and impressive, even in the many texts in which he described the physical environment. Two fundamental forms of opening description are particularly significant in their relationship to the reader's grasp and elaboration of the text. The first is the realistic description, purported to represent faithfully the reality described. This type of description is based on an illusion of absolute objectivity, of the author's ability to duplicate a milieu exterior to the text itself. These are plentiful in Balzac's work, and they deserve our close attention because they dictate a specific and significant form of contact between text and reader. Clearly, the realistic description was an important element in Balzac's style and philosophy of composition. Its importance, I would argue, is based on its relational value within the text. As our point of entry, it relates reader to text. As representation of an environment, it relates milieu to the events and the characters of the story. The realistic description is thus the textual pivot upon which turn reader and tale, the door through which we enter, the map by which we interpret. The second form of description shares a number of these characteristics, yet it exerts a different control over our reading. The abstract description is not founded in an illusion of objectivity; instead, the narrator subjectively abstracts, interprets, or reduces for us an object or a milieu too large, too grand, or too dynamic to be seized by the naked eye. The abstract description relies heavily upon poetic images to capture the essence of what is being described (here, the city of Paris), so that the author might offer us a milieu in a concentrated form. The more vivid the images that compose the description, the more successfully will we be drawn into the creation of a seemingly physical milieu. The intellectual approach of the realistic description thus gives way to an emotional and poetic appeal.

The Realistic Description

Nineteenth-century France, by its very dynamism, offered novelists new challenges. Fictional portrayal of the turbulent social scene required that the author experiment with new strategies and literary techniques. Robert Alter interpreted the lengthy descriptions of *La Comédie humaine* (and those of other nineteenth-century writers) as the means by which the author explored the relationship between reality and the "real-seeming artifice." Alter related the development of the realistic description in nineteenth-century fiction to the "crisis in traditional literature reflected in the very emergence of the novel as a new genre." During this time, according to Alter, the center of attention within the novel shifted "to the world around and how it impinged with its specific gravity, its full concreteness, on consciousness."[13] The study of the "world around" and its relationship to the individual and society was important to Balzac, but the means of portraying it to an active reader was as well. In Alter's opinion, the novel form provided Balzac and others the vehicle in which to contain reality and, beyond that, to compete with it:

> Psychologically, novel-writing was seized as a means of containing the mounting chaos of the contemporary world, recasting it in the molds of the imagination and thus transforming it, even as the deadly weight of its real menace was still felt in the finished fiction. If the novel, then, was in one aspect an embracing representation of contemporary society, it was also conceived as a vigorous competitor to the reality it was supposed to represent.[14]

We know that Balzac set as a goal that very competition. But what seems even more significant in Balzac's use of description, and perhaps in his work in general, was his concentration upon the art form. Although it necessarily reflected the outside world, the reality that he created was of the narration itself. And it is in the context of the structure and functioning of narrative elements that the description, realistic or abstract, must be studied.

As Pierre Laubriet has established in *L'Intelligence de l'art chez Balzac*, Balzac saw as the mission of art the translation of the most profound truths of nature. Laubriet defines the concept in this way:

Le vrai balzacien . . . n'est pas . . . la reproduction inchangée du réel offert par la nature; cette peinture exacte . . . n'est ni souhaitable, car le vrai de la nature s'écarte trop souvent du vrai littéraire par manque d'unité, par défaut de vraisemblance, ni possible, car le vrai littéraire est toujours une reconstruction de la nature par une intelligence, un tempérament qui en offre une synthèse forcément déformée. Le vrai est toujours transposé. Bien plus, il apparaît comme une nécessité inhérente à l'oeuvre d'art que le vrai de la nature soit idéalisé et spiritualisé.[15]

(Balzacian truth . . . is not . . . the unchanged reproduction of the reality of nature; such exact painting is neither desirable since the truth of nature deviates too often from literary truth by its lack of unity or its lack of verisimilitude, nor possible since literary truth is always a reconstruction of nature by intelligence, by temperament that offers a necessarily deformed synthesis of it. Truth is always transposed. Furthermore, it appears inherently necessary in the work of art that the truth of nature be idealized and spiritualized.)

It was, however, through fidelity to the physical or observable nature of reality that literature, and thus the description, could grasp the essence of that reality, could transcend the observable to perceive or to intuit more profound levels of truth. The visible yielded to the invisible through both the astute observation of the author and his skillful artistic rendering of insight. It was upon these ideas that Balzac based his concept of artistic genius, a dual process that replaced long scientific inquiry with an intuitive grasp of the truth, a grasp that took observation as its starting point.[16] The second phase of the process, the expression of that truth in literary terms, was the domain in which the description was of particular importance. Balzac's seeming faithfulness to a reality exterior to the novel, his creation within the text of a reality that patterns the exterior duality, and his efforts to penetrate the observable surface are more clear in the description than they are in other segments of narration. It was his constant search for "le vrai" and for the means to represent it adequately in the novel that led him to his experimentation with the description. In the description, Balzac presented the two phases of the artistic process. Not only did he offer us an artistic rendering of the truth as he perceived it (in all its dynamism and contrariness), but he showed as well the very process of observation, the moments of insight, and the questioning that took him beyond the surface. In other words, the reader stands in relation to the description as Balzac stood in relation to an exterior reality, and Balzac has called upon us to follow his lead and to apply our own intuitive powers to the reality of that description in order to evolve with him the more profound layers of meaning coded within. Thus, although the relationship between the description and an actual reality exterior to the text may have been significant for Balzac—as both observer and artist—and I would by no means argue that it always was, it is of far less importance to us as readers. The only reality with which we must be concerned is that of the description itself. The descriptive technique that presents the dual artistic process focuses our attention on the passage itself and makes the reading of the description an artistic operation parallel to its composition. The description, which so often seems to duplicate that which was tangible and solid in the author's actual world, functions principally as a means to ground and orient us in the narration, to color, if not form, our interpretation of it, and to dictate to us the guidelines for our creative participation in Balzac's fiction.

La Recherche de l'absolu begins with the following description, an example of what many would call a typical Balzacian opening.

> Il existe à Douai dans la rue de Paris une maison dont la physionomie, les dispositions intérieures et les détails ont, plus que ceux d'aucun autre logis, gardé le caractère des vieilles construction [sic] flamandes, si naïvement appropriées aux moeurs patriarcales de ce bon pays. (10:657)

> (There exists in Douai, in the Rue de Paris, a house that by outward appearance, interior arrangement, and details has, more than all others in the city, maintained the character of old Flemish constructions, so thoroughly in keeping with the patriarchal manners of that good country.)

That the house to be described is characteristic of Flemish architecture invites us to begin visualizing it even while we are assured of the narrator's objectivity. This fragment of a sentence, which entices us by the potential it offers for mimesis and for the transparent language of referentiality (in other words, for reality), is undercut immediately by the second portion of the sentence:

> mais avant de la décrire, peut-être faut-il établir dans l'intérêt des écrivains la nécessité de ces préparations didactiques contre lesquelles protestent certaines personnes ignorantes et voraces qui voudraient des émotions sans en subir les principes générateurs, la fleur sans la graine, l'enfant sans la gestation. (10:657)

> (But before describing it, perhaps I ought to establish, on behalf of authors, the need for these didactic preliminaries that certain ignorant and impatient people protest. There are those who would wish emotions without submitting themselves to the influences that produce them, who would have the flower without the seed, the child without gestation.)

As readers, we are snatched abruptly from the description, and from the world of referentiality as well, then thrust into a closer, more direct communication with the author and into the world of textuality. The first sentence begins as description but is in fact the opening to a lengthy defense of the description, a response to criticism Balzac had received on his use of that technique,[17] and a statement of the narrative and artistic function of the description in literature. The statement of purpose is significant for what it says about the creative process of the author, but it is even more so for what it says about our function vis-à-vis the description and its relation to our interpretation of the narration. Balzac included the defense in the interest of writers (himself, of course) and attempted to clear up a misunderstanding that had negatively affected the reception of his works. Interestingly, although he labeled the openings as "didactic preliminaries," he also declared them to be essential to his narration (to its success vis-à-vis the reader and the author, we might assume). Clearly, from Balzac's point of view, the description is directly tied to the readers, is designed to inform them of and prepare them for the action to come. More than a part of the action itself, the description serves as a prelude in which the readers are positioned in relation to the narration.

From such statements of principle as are included in *La Recherche de l'absolu* and in the preface to *Une Fille d'Eve*, we see the description taking on at least two different roles in relation to the reader and the narration. In the latter novel, Balzac's stated goal is purely a didactic one; he sought to inform his readers of what they needed to know in order to grasp the story. He blamed the long documentation of the description on the "excessive ambition" of the author who wished only "peindre le pays" ("to portray the country") and "raconter les plus beaux sites et les principales villes de la France aux étrangers, constater l'état des constructions anciennes et modernes au dix-neuvième siècle"(2:267) ("to tell foreigners of the most beautiful sites and principal cities of France, to establish the state of old as well as modern structures in the nineteenth century"). But in *La Recherche de l'absolu*, he embellished his statement of goals considerably by addressing himself to the more complicated questions of narrative technique and of the relationship between the narrative and the actuality that it represents.

Les événements de la vie humaine, soit publique, soit privée, sont si intimement liés à l'architecture, que la plupart des observateurs peuvent reconstruire les nations ou les individus dans toute la vérité de leurs habitudes, d'après les restes de leurs monuments publics ou par l'examen de leurs reliques domestiques. L'archéologie est à la nature sociale ce que l'anatomie comparée est à la nature organisée. Une mosaïque révèle toute une société, comme un squelette d'ichthyosaure sous-entend toute une création. De part et d'autre, tout se déduit, tout s'enchaîne. La cause fait deviner un effet, comme chaque effet permet de remonter à une cause. Le savant ressuscite ainsi jusqu'aux verrues des vieux âges. De là vient sans doute le prodigieux intérêt qu'inspire une description architecturale quand la fantaisie de l'écrivain n'en dénature point les éléments; chacun ne peut-il pas la rattacher au passé par de sévères déductions; et, pour l'homme, le passé ressemble singulièrement à l'avenir: lui raconter ce qui fut, n'est-ce pas presque toujours lui dire ce qui sera? Enfin, il est rare que la peinture des lieux où la vie s'écoule ne rappelle à chacun ou ses voeux trahis ou ses espérances en fleur. La comparaison entre un présent qui trompe les vouloirs secrets et l'avenir qui peut les réaliser est une source inépuisable de mélancolie ou de satisfactions douces. Aussi est-il presque impossible de ne pas être pris d'une espèce d'attendrissement à la peinture de la vie flamande, quand les accessoires en sont bien rendus. (10:657–58)

(Both public and private events of human life are so intimately linked to architecture that most observers can reconstruct the truth of nations or individuals in all their habits by examining the remains of their public monuments or of their domestic life. Archaeology is to society what comparative anatomy is to organized nature. A mosaic reveals an entire society just as a skeleton of an ichthyosaurus implies a whole past order of things. Everything is understandable, everything is linked. The cause implies the effect as every effect permits us to grasp the cause. Thus the scientist brings to life whole past ages down to the very warts. Hence, no doubt, the prodigious interest that an architectural description arouses, as long as the author does not distort the elements; cannot we all call up the past for ourselves by the process of deduction? And for man, the past strangely resembles the future; to tell him what was is almost to tell him what will be, is it not? As a matter of fact, it is rare that the description of a place where the current of life flows not recall to each either his broken resolutions or his budding hopes. Comparison between the present that disappoints our secret wishes and the future that can fulfill them is an inexhaustible source of sadness or sweet satisfaction. Thus it is almost impossible not to be a little touched by the description of Flemish life, when the details are faithfully rendered.)

Balzac spoke to us not only of himself as observer but also of the possibilities that observation offers for the perception and creation of both meaning and relationships between the container and the contained, the milieu and the event, the structure and the structured. It is even more interesting to note that this passage also directs us rather explicitly on how to receive and manipulate the lengthy descriptions within Balzac's narrations. He did not link the description of the setting to actual historical events but to narrative ones, for the description is no more than a narrative element. As relationships exist in nature and in society, so do they exist in the literary text; they are not reproductions of the natural or societal, but they are faithful to them in their dynamics. As archaeology reveals social nature and as comparative anatomy reveals physical nature, so does the description reveal the dynamics of the narration and the nature of the tale to be told. Our task, then, is clear. We are to deduce meaning as scientific observers do; we are to follow their methods and to create within the narration itself relationships representative of those within nature and society.[18] And the description will be designed to facilitate that activity.

As it links us as readers to the narration, the description will also inadvertently link us to the exterior reality upon which the narration is patterned. The author must then be faithful in the description to the exterior reality that it represents: "De là vient sans doute le prodigieux intérêt qu'inspire une description architecturale quand la fantaisie de l'écrivain n'en dénature point les éléments" ("Hence, no doubt, the prodigious interest that an architectural description arouses, as long as the author does not distort the elements"). By its seeming duplication of reality, its "vraisemblance," the opening description becomes the transition for us as readers and for the author himself from the reality of an actual environment to that of the narration. Through the opening description, we enter definitively into the narrative world. Of course, the opening description, although it may be related to an exterior environment, is itself fully a part of the narration. Actual duplication of reality is not essential to the successful functioning of the description; only the pretense of that duplication is needed. In fact, as Madeleine Fargeaud pointed out in her introduction to La Recherche de l'absolu, only the names used in the description of the "maison douaisienne" are authentically Flemish. Instead, the description is based on "vraisemblance locale et vérité provinciale, vérité typique" (10:645)[19] ("local probability and provincial truth, representative truth"). Coded within that description are indications of the nature of relationships to be established within the narration, as well as guidelines for the activity that will establish them. The appearance of duplication places us on firm and familiar ground and thus helps us to decode the description in its relationship to the rest of the text: "le vraisemblable est le masque dont s'affublent les lois du texte, et que nous sommes censés prendre pour une relation avec la réalité"[20] ("the Probable is the mask with which the laws of the text disguise themselves and that we are supposed to take for a relation with reality"). Thus the description fosters an illusion of reality by serving as the transition between two separate but related domains and by engaging us as the mediators or actualizers of the transition.

> *Chaque oeuvre d'art présente, dans une indécomposable unité, un double caractère: elle exprime la réalité mais lui donne forme aussi bien; la réalité n'est donc pas à côté de l'oeuvre ou hors d'elle mais n'existe que dans l'oeuvre. L'oeuvre d'art n'est pas l'illustration de représentations à propos de la réalité. Comme oeuvre et comme art, elle pro-pose la réalité et par là, indissolublement lui donne forme.*[21]

> (Every work of art presents a double character in indecomposable unity: it represents reality but also gives it its form. Reality is not, therefore, beside the work or outside of it but exists only in it. The work of art is not the illustration of representations in connection with reality. As work and as art, it pro-poses reality and thereby indissolubly gives it form.)

The duplication thus becomes as well the means by which the author guides our interpretation and our comprehension of what is about to unfold in the milieu described. At the same time, however, it is clear from the final portion of the Balzacian passage cited above that Balzac understood that the reader's response is essentially subjective and therefore not entirely controllable. He seems to have acknowledged what reader-response theorists tell us today, that the reception and the interpretation of a narration, and thus of a description, will be formed by our deepest recesses ("ses voeux trahis ou ses espérances en fleur"). This passage then demonstrates Balzac's interest in the description as a singularly important element uniting reader and text. Because he acknowledged the subjectivity of reader response, it is not surprising that he rarely left solely to the imagination of the reader the grasp of a descriptive element essential to the comprehension of an event. Each part of the opening description of *La Recherche de l'absolu* is marked by the author's concern that his reader be correctly positioned for the reception of the text.

Following the blatant defense of his technique (cited above), Balzac changed his approach somewhat. Having announced, "Aussi est-il presque impossible de ne pas être pris d'une espèce d'attendrissement à la peinture de la vie flamande, quand les accessoires en sont bien rendus" ("Thus it is almost impossible not to be a little touched by the description of Flemish life when the details are faithfully rendered"), he turned not to a presentation of those details but to an attempt to ensure the emotional response. In a long passage (three pages), he praised the Flemish, touching on everything from family life to national character, from the predominant colors of the landscape to the place of Flanders within the nineteenth-century European political and commercial structure, from the nature of Flemish art to the importance of tobacco in Flemish society. There is little left to chance as each item mentioned is interpreted for us by the narrator. We are, in effect, being given the tone, if not the information, with which to interpret both the description of the house and all that it implies for those within. Throughout this long passage, which is designed to fill in the background of the story and to dispose us to it positively by the narrator's tone and interpretation, we are reminded that it is to a narration and not to actual events that the passage applies. Twice, references are made to the description promised in the first sentence of the novel, keeping that description before us as a future event of our reading and reminding us that we are the recipients of a narration: "Mais les douces poésies de cette vie patriarcale se retrouveront naturellement dans la peinture d'une des dernières maisons qui, au temps où cette histoire commence, en conservaient encore ... " (10:661) ("But the grace and poetry of this patriarchal existence will be naturally revealed in a description of one of the last remaining houses, which at the time when this story begins, still preserved ..."). Each reference merely returns us to the opening lines of the narration, repeating the information and promising once again the description of the house that has become so important; the author has made clear to us its role within his narration and ours in relation to it. But the narrator does not immediately produce it. Yet another paragraph turns our attention to the city of Douai before we at last read, "La maison où se sont passés les événements de cette histoire se trouve à peu près au milieu de la rue de Paris, et porte à

Douai, depuis plus de deux cents ans, le nom de la Maison Claës" (10:661) ("The house in which the events of this story took place, is located approximately halfway down the Rue de Paris, and has borne in Douai, for more than two hundred years, the name of the Maison Claës"). Here, the detailed description of the house begins.

The entire first section of *La Recherche de l'absolu*, which comments on and clearly builds up to a description of milieu, is designed to position us as readers not so much within the cultural and historical moment as within Balzac's narration. It dictates to us a positive attitude toward the author's choice of technique and toward the house to be described. It molds our attitude toward the author, his authoritative and seemingly objective narrator, and the characters who have not yet entered the scene. At the same time, both by direct statement and by the implication of the effort to influence our response, it acknowledges the essentially subjective nature of that response. Even before the description gets fully under way in the narration, the foundation for its successful functioning has been laid.

I maintain that the sort of material we find in the opening of *La Recherche de l'absolu*, as well as the descriptions themselves, do not point to an author overwhelmed by the reality that he portrays (as Robert Alter seems to imply), but clearly to one in control of it. Furthermore, they demonstrate that Balzac was conscious of his art. From the opening of *La Recherche de l'absolu*, we see the approach that the author used in creating the description, the significance of the choice of details it was to contain, and the important function of the active reader in relating the description to the rest of the narration and in elaborating its symbolic value.

The Balzacian description belongs to what Peter Brooks in *The Melodramatic Imagination* has called the "world of hypersignificant signs,"[22] and it requires our interpretation lest we be overwhelmed by its weight and detail. Neither the realistic nor the abstract description is based on a strict word-object relationship but on one that relates the word to the narrative object or event through the work of the active reader: a relationship that engages the reader in an activity essential to the comprehension and elaboration of the text. Brooks maintained that much of Balzac's writing is symbolic, that it, like all else "on the surface," stood for something larger and beyond. In his analysis, the object of Balzac's aesthetic was

> to make the plane of representation imply, suggest, open onto the world of spirit as much as can possibly be managed; to make the vehicles of representation evocative of significant tenors. Meaning is ever conceived as latent; description of surface will not necessarily and of itself give access to the inner world of significance. Hence the "pressure" applied to the surfaces of the real, the insistence of the recording glance, striving toward that moment where as Albert Béguin has put it "vision becomes vision."[23]

The "pressure" to which he refers, the narrator's frequent questioning of his own narration or the implication that a given detail is replete with hidden meaning, offers us, in and of itself, a model of appropriate reading. It suggests, of course, that we follow suit and challenges us to go beyond the surface detail—which will be rendered faithfully and objectively by the narrator—toward interpretation. The fictional reality that the reader creates within the narration and through the symbolic language of the description is as broad as that reader is able to make it while following the author's guidelines. Although the guidelines within the realistic description may be quite different from those within the abstract, the task of the reader remains the same, as does the narrative function of the description.

From the author's point of view, the realistic description in *La Recherche de l'absolu*, more than the abstract, depends upon visual perception or the memory of it. With its famous detail (of color, texture, and depth, for example), the realistic description should evoke within us a similar visual perception. The reader's perception is, of course, only metaphorically visual, which is appropriate given the symbolic value of the language and the fictionality of the reality being created. The vividness of the description within the narration and its evocative power vis-à-vis other narrative elements are contingent upon our accepting the illusion of visual perception and our participating in it, actions that permit our becoming fixed in relation to the narrative to follow. These actions, moreover, effect the transition from that which is outside the text to that which is inside it, a transition contained only potentially within the description itself. The reception of the realistic opening description is, then, the most important moment of our reading. Through the description, more particularly through the objective narrator and our participation in the illusion of reality, Balzac implanted impressions that become significant as we progress in our reading. Through the technique of the realistic description, we are induced to see what is described and to believe that what we see is real. Because a code that will color our interpretation of the text is also communicated to us through the description, the opening positions us in relation to the entire narration and prepares us for our reception of the dynamic structure of the novel. By its very nature, then, and certainly by the role that it plays within the text, the realistic description (and to a lesser degree the abstract description as well) is a means by which Balzac exerted a significant measure of control over the reception of his narration.

The opening description in *La Recherche de l'absolu* fulfills Balzac's goal perhaps more thoroughly than do other openings, with its three false starts. Each signals a narrowing of our field of vision or a specific focusing of our attention (from general commentary on the description to a discussion of Flemish national character, to a description of the city of Douai, to a brief family history, and finally to the house itself). The actual description of the house is thus preceded by a wealth of information on the people, the area, and the family, allowing us to visualize and interpret the house itself more acutely. Furthermore, the interrelatedness of the background information and the actual description is reinforced by the highly directive narrator, as in the following passage. "La constante honnêteté, la loyauté sans tache des Claës, leur invariable décorum faisaient d'eux une superstition aussi invétérée que celle de la fête de Gayant, et bien exprimée par ce nom, la Maison Claës" (10:663) ("The unswerving loyalty, the spotless integrity of the Claës, together with their staid, impressive demeanor under all circumstances, had given rise to a sort of legend of the Claës, and the Maison Claës was as much an institution in the city as the Fête de Gayant"). It is hard to imagine how we could be more prepared for this description; the author has discussed its function, the manner in which we are to receive it, and the background information that shaped it. Finally, armed with instruction and aware of its purpose, we are faced with the description that has been promised and referred to throughout six pages of narration.

The actual description delineates the façade of the house, using as its starting point the feature that ostensibly first catches the eye, the door: "Le principal ornement de la façade était une porte à deux vantaux en chêne garnis de clous disposés en quinconce, au centre desquels les Claës avaient fait sculpter par orgueil deux navettes accouplées" (10:663) ("The principal ornament of the house front was the great doorway with its folding leaves of oak, studded with large nails, arranged in groups of five; in the center the Claës had proudly carved their arms, two spindles conjoined"). The progression of the description follows the narrator's eye as he objectively details all that surrounds the door—windows, walls, bricks, and mortar—with emphasis on color, depth, and texture. As if to emphasize the relationship that he has discussed somewhat philosophically in the opening, the narrator gives significance even to the fact that the smallest details on the façade are perceptible, establishing the relationship of that fact to the characters inside the house: "Quoique le temps eût jeté sa teinte sur les travaux délicats de cette porte et de la lanterne, le soin extrême qu'en prenaient les gens du logis permettait aux passants d'en saisir tous les détails" (10:663) ("The delicate carving about the shrine and the doorway had grown somewhat darker by the lapse of time; but so carefully had it been kept by the owners of the house, that every detail was visible to a passerby"). This highly economic sentence reinforces the author's claim of objectivity and realism, defends once again his technique for the description, and illustrates to us further the ways in which details of the milieu have meaning when applied to characters of the story.

Although the material that forms the basis of our interpretation of the relationship between the house's façade and the family within (the context of national, urban, and family history) largely precedes the actual description, it is this linkage of architecture to people that, according to Madeleine Fargeaud, renders the description three-dimensional:

> en projetant sur les choses l'éclairage des intentions humaines, Balzac a donné vie et relief aux détails décrits. La maison, primitivement contemplée de l'extérieur, est vue de l'intérieur par l'auteur et prend ainsi tout naturellement sa place dans l'espace et le temps. Liée aux hommes, elle a acquis un sens historique, et porte la marque du lent devenir des choses.[24]

> (in projecting the illumination of human intentions on things, Balzac has given life and texture to those details described. The house, originally contemplated from the outside, is seen from the interior by the author and takes its place quite naturally in that way in space and in time. Linked to men as it is, it has acquired an historical meaning and carries the mark of the slow development of things.)

The description stresses the relationship not only between the house and its occupants but also between itself and its narrator. Rather than an objective representation of the façade, we read a subjective summarization of the narrator's impression of it, which emphasizes both the narrator's role and ours and which molds our interpretation: "Aussi le fini, l'air propre de cette façade à demi râpée par le frottement lui donnaient-ils un aspect sèchement honnête et décemment estimable, qui, certes, aurait fait déménager un romantique, s'il eût logé en face" (10:664) ("There was an excessive neatness and smoothness about the house front, worn with repeated scourings; an air of sedate propriety and of grim respectability that would have driven a romantic away if he lived across the street").

Having backed away from the house for an overall and subjective response, the narrator approaches the door once again to look even more closely and visually enters the house by looking through a window. The description of the interior has none of the detail given for the façade. The narrator reports to us only what the eye would perceive through the window of the door, principally the arrangement of the rooms. Again, there is little interpretation except to say that the pattern of light reflected gives it all "une grâce mystérieuse et de fantastiques apparences" (10:665) ("a mysterious charm and a fantastic look").

Thus far in the description, Balzac has restrained his narrator by limiting blatant interpretation and has left to us the task of incorporating the image of the house into the background information we have been supplied. In the second phase of the description, however, his control of our activity has been more subtly incorporated into the description, and the direction our interpretation will take has been determined. The narrator's eye penetrates the façade to the family quarters where the same details are recorded (door, windows, room arrangement, and lighting). With the announcement that one room is of particular significance to the family a new and more subtle form of description is begun: "mais rien ne pouvait égaler aux yeux des Claës, ni au jugement d'un connaisseur, les trésors qui ornaient cette pièce, où, depuis deux siècles, s'était écoulée la vie de la famille" (10:665) ("But nothing, in the eyes of Claës or in the judgment of a connoisseur, could compare to the art treasures that decorated this room that had been the center of family life for two centuries"). Our attention, heightened by the signal, is sharply focused on each objet d'art within the finely decorated room. The seeming objectivity of the narrator is abandoned for more self-conscious and subjective narration. The process is as follows: each detail of the description is linked to an aspect of the family's life, with regular alternation between the two levels of the narration (objective description, family history) and between two activities of both author and reader (observation, intuition of meaning). The passage glides smoothly between these two activities, forcing us to link each object with some element of family history. The description of this all-important room, the center of activity for the narration, is based on the very dynamic that Balzac has attributed to description as a narrative element. He did not leave to us the task of deducing the cause from the effect or the effect from the cause, having clearly spelled out the essence of the links between object and character or event, links that are essential to our successful interpretation of the relationship between description and other narrative elements. The process of alternation between the description of the object and the explanation of its history can be demonstrated by the following segment of the description.

Le Claës mort pour la cause des libertés gantoises, l'artisan de qui l'on prendrait une trop mince idée, si l'historien omettait de dire qu'il possédait près de quarante mille marcs d'argent, gagnés dans la fabrication des voiles nécessaires à la toute puissante marine vénitienne; ce Claës eut pour ami le célèbre sculpteur en bois Van Huysium de Bruges. Maintes fois, l'artiste avait puisé dans la bourse de l'artisan. Quelque temps avant la révolte des Gantois, Van Huysium, devenu riche, avait secrètment sculpté pour son ami une boiserie en ébène massif où étaient représentées les principales scènes de la vie d'Artevelde, ce brasseur, un moment roi des Flandres. Ce revêtement, composé de soixante panneaux, contenait environ quatorze cents personnages principaux, et passait pour l'oeuvre capitale de Van Huysium. Le capitaine chargé de garder les bourgeois que Charles-Quint avait décidé de faire pendre le jour de son entrée dans sa ville natale proposa, dit-on, à Van Claës de le laisser évader s'il lui donnait l'oeuvre de Van Huysium; mais le tisserand l'avait envoyée en France. Ce parloir, entièrement boisé avec ces panneaux que, par respect pour les mânes du martyr, Van Huysium vint lui-même encadrer de bois peint en outremer mélangé de filets d'or, est donc l'oeuvre la plus complète de ce maître, dont aujourd'hui les moindres morceaux sont payés presque au poids de l'or. (10:665–66)

(The historian should not omit to record of the Claës who died for the cause of freedom in Ghent, that he had accumulated nearly forty thousand silver marks, gained by the manufacture of sailcloths for the all-powerful navy of Venice. The Flemish craftsman was a man of substance and had for a friend the celebrated woodcarver, Van Huysium, of Bruges. Many times the artist had dipped into his friend's funds. When Ghent rose in revolt, Van Huysium, then himself a wealthy man, had secretly carved for his old friend a piece of paneling of massive ebony, on which he portrayed the story of Van Artevelde, the brewer who for a little while ruled over Flanders. This piece of woodwork consisted of sixty panels and contained about fourteen hundred figures; it was considered to be Van Huysium's masterpiece.

When Charles V made up his mind to celebrate his entry into the city that gave him birth by hanging twenty-six of its burghers, the victims were placed in the custody of a captain, who (so it was said) had offered to let Claës escape in return for these panels of Van Huysium's, but the weaver had previously sent them into France.

The parlor in the house in the Rue de Paris was wainscoted entirely with these panels. Van Huysium, out of respect for the memory of the martyr, had come himself to set them in their wooden framework, painted with ultramarine, and covered with a gilded network, so that this is the most complete example of a master whose least fragments are now worth their weight in gold.)

Although with perhaps less historic detail, each object falling within the narrator's view and within the purview of his narration is similarly treated. He places each object in its historical context, bringing us chronologically to the narrative present of *La Recherche de l'absolu*. We are led into the very activity that has been delineated within the text as that appropriate to the recipient of the description. The historical relationship of setting to event is established for us in order that we may participate more actively in a similar creation of relationships in the narration to come.

Having made his tour of the room and its contents, the narrator concludes his description, indeed cuts it short: "Il est inutile de continuer la description de la Maison Claës dans les autres parties de laquelle se passeront nécessairement plusieurs scènes de cette histoire, il suffit, en ce moment, d'en connaître les principales dispositions" (10:667) ("It is unnecessary to describe the Maison Claës at further length. Many of the scenes in the course of this story will, of course, take place in other parts of the house, but it will be sufficient for the present to have some idea of its general arrangement"). This sentence reinforces the utilitarian aspect of the description in its relation to the rest of the narration and to readers. It reinforces as well our position as recipients of the narration and that of the narrator as the controlling agent in its presentation. The implication of this terminating sentence, of course, is that we will be informed only of what we need to grasp and to interpret the narration. More knowledge would perhaps lessen the author's control over our shaping of the text. Too little would also lessen his control, because we would not be adequately conditioned for what is to come.

Throughout the whole presentation, the presence of the

narrator can be strongly felt, and, as the above-cited sentence illustrates, information about the milieu of the tale has been carefully doled out. Peter Brooks accounted for the "dominating presence of the narrator" by relating it to the implicit hidden meaning that is part of all Balzacian surface representation. To indicate the presence of hidden meaning and to direct us to it, claimed Brooks, Balzac interjected the narrator—who weaves a "tissue of explanatory references"—between us and a level of signification only symbolized by the surface.[25] This "tissue" is particularly clear in the description of the "maison douaisienne," alternating as it does between a past and a present and focusing the eye of the reader at every turn on the object of greatest symbolic value. The process contributes to the generation of an illusion of reality. The dominating presence of the narrator, however, controls that illusion by creating one of broader impact, that of a performance, the illusion that the description is being recounted to us. For later authors of the nineteenth century, the illusion of reality was lost if the author showed his hand as Balzac did throughout this description. But, in fact, the performative aspect of the narrator's presence, and the clear role that it dictates to us, makes possible a different sense of reality, one that clearly exists within an artistic framework and that is defined by it. If the performace of the narrator is successful and if we agree to play our role as audience, a rather complex illusion of reality will be created through the interaction between the two. The seeming objectivity of the narrator, the control of our knowledge, and the alternation between object and an explanation of its import all contribute to the illusions that make the realistic opening description in *La Recherche de l'absolu* effective, an ideal narrative element through which to enter into the narration.

The opening of *La Recherche de l'absolu* offers us, then, not only an excellent example of the realistic description in Balzac's work but the author's commentary on its function and importance as well. The description itself and all the material introducing it chart an appropriate reception of the narration for the reader. The shaping of our response is effected through the intersection of numerous aspects of the

description: its direct appeal to us; the raw material of interpretation that it furnishes; the seeming objectivity of the
narrator combined with his domination of the narration; and
the structure of the description, linking present to past and
object to event. All of this, of course, precedes the entrance of
the characters. We are therefore prepared by this description
not only for their entrance and the events of their story but
also for our role as audience. The description has momentarily suspended our reading in order to orient and to direct us. It
is, I believe, the moment in which Balzac exerts his greatest
control over us, making the realistic opening description as
significant to our understanding of Balzac's process of writing
as it is to our grasp of the process of reading.

The Abstract Description

Not all descriptions in *La Comédie humaine* are so clearly
manipulative of the reader's response, nor are they so clear in
their manner of presentation. The second form of description
to be considered here, the abstract description, which has as
its object an entity too large, broad, or dynamic to be captured
by the narrator's eye (thus rendering inadequate the mimetic
technique of the realistic description), poses a different challenge to the author and to the reader alike. Given the number
of times that the city of Paris is represented in *La Comédie
humaine,* we might assume that the problem of its description arose repeatedly. The technique that Balzac chose on numerous occasions was a narrator caught up in the spectacle
before him and responding subjectively to it. The abstract
description relies heavily upon images and poetic language
and is filled with interpretation. Organized for an emotional
rather than an intellectual impact, these descriptions enable
the readers to sense the aura that surrounds the milieu or the
impression that it leaves, rather than to create the illusion of
perception. In a much more blatant way than in the realistic
description, texture, color, and depth are given moral or emotional significance. The surface described barely counts or
counts exclusively for its symbolic value, seized upon only as

an evocation of a far greater reality. The more each detail can be made to resonate with meaning, the better can a large and dynamic whole be evoked. This type of description does not reflect an effort to duplicate an exterior reality; instead, the description reduces or abstracts it, portraying the essence of its dynamism, a sort of raw dynamism. As readers, we are not carefully positioned in relation to the action to come, but thrust into it, interjected into the milieu already in motion. Although the two forms of description approach the object described in radically different ways, much of what Balzac said in *La Recherche de l'absolu* about the role of the description within a narration applies equally here. But to link so vast a milieu to the events that take place within it, to evoke the relationships between an entity so large as Paris and another so particular as the story of a few individuals, and at the same time to allow us to maintain an illusion of reality, the description must be differently presented and our reception of it shaped in quite different ways.

Ferragus, the first part of the trilogy *Histoire des Treize* (followed by *La Duchesse de Langeais* and *La Fille aux yeux d'or*), opens with just such an evocation of Paris. It is only one of the many stories that take as their subject the secret societies with which we know Balzac was fascinated. As he has told us in *La Recherche de l'absolu* that it should, the opening description of *Ferragus* reflects not only the vastness of the milieu that it describes but also the nature and structure of the events to take place there.

Rose Fortassier, in her introduction to the 1977 Pléiade edition of the trilogy, claimed that the image of association that the secret society represented blended with Balzac's own dream of "toute-puissance" ("all-powerfulness"): "par une union où chacun se met inconditionnellement au service des autres, l'individu multiplie son pouvoir; le pacte d'alliance fait de lui 'un homme plus grand que les hommes' " (5:739) ("by an association in which everyone places himself unconditionally in the service of the others, the individual multiplies his power; the agreement makes of him 'a man greater than men' "). The subject matter uniting the three tales is that of secrecy and mystery, of invisible links and forces, of the fantasy of power and the strength of fraternity. Balzac himself described the "Société des Treize" ("The Thirteen") in these terms: "leur puissance occulte, contre laquelle l'ordre social serait sans défense, y renverserait les obstacles, foudroierait les volontés, et donnerait à chacun d'eux le pouvoir diabolique de tous" (5:791) ("their hidden might, against which the social order would have no defense, would overturn obstacles, paralyze their opponents' wills and confer their collective power on each individual member"[26]). The society, he adds, "fut horrible et sublime" (5:792) ("was at once horrible and sublime," p. 26). How to evoke the setting of such an organization, of such movement and dynamism, how to create a landscape worthy of the events to unfurl and the society contained in *Ferragus* was the challenge that Balzac faced. The landscape he chose, of course, was his own Paris, and Rose Fortassier claimed that Paris itself is a major theme in the trilogy. She saw in this theme not only the setting for the action but also the unity of the three narrations. That the cadre of the terrible events in *Histoire des Treize* should be the unifying feature of the narrations is consistent with the importance that Balzac has attributed to setting and to description in *La Recherche de l'absolu*. Fortassier proposed as well that it was the work of James Fenimore Cooper *(The Last of the Mohicans, The Pioneers, The Prairie)* that influenced Balzac's choice of a triadic structure for this series of narrations.[27] Yet it was the description of landscape and setting that Balzac seems to have most admired in the American author.

Balzac ended his preface to *Histoire des Treize* by telling us that he could then begin "le récit des trois épisodes qui, dans cette histoire, l'ont particulièrement séduit par la senteur parisienne des détails, et par la bizarrerie des contrastes" (5:792) ("his narration of the three episodes of this history which he himself found especially attractive because of the Parisian flavor of the details and the strange contrasts they reveal," p. 27). *Ferragus* then opens with an evocation of Parisian streets, which from its first words is heavy with the narrator's moral interpretations of all that is seen. Unlike the

description of the "maison douaisienne," based on the steady
and objective eye of the narrator, this passage progresses by
leaps from contrast to contrast and from neighborhood to
neighborhood. The narrator evokes and interprets as economically as possible, as the opening sentence illustrates:

> Il est dans Paris certaines rues déshonorées autant que peut
> l'être un homme coupable d'infamie; puis il existe des rues no-
> bles, puis des rues simplement honnêtes, puis de jeunes rues sur
> la moralité desquelles le public ne s'est pas encore formé d'opinion;
> puis des rues assassines, des rues plus vieilles que de vieilles
> douairières ne sont vieilles, des rues estimables, des rues toujours
> propres, des rues toujours sales, des rues ouvrières, travailleuses,
> mercantiles. (5:793)

> (In Paris there are certain streets which are in as much disrepute
> as any man branded with infamy can be. There are also noble
> streets; then there are streets which are just simply decent, and, so
> to speak adolescent streets about whose morality the public has
> not yet formed an opinion. There are murderous streets; streets
> which are more aged than aged dowagers; respectable streets;
> streets which are always clean; streets which are always dirty;
> working-class, industrious, mercantile streets.) (p. 31)

The technique to be used in the description is clearly marked
in the first sentence. We are assailed with adjectives, with the
attribution of moral qualities to the streets and in turn to
their inhabitants, with the juxtaposition of contrasts, with
the detailing of nuances of difference, and with the accumulation and rapid delivery of words. The combination communicates movement, lack of visible organization, and an accelerated rhythm into which the reader is thrust. At the same
time, the evocation of so many different kinds of streets
permitted Balzac to begin immediately to reduce and to abstract the Paris to be described. The accelerated rhythm and
the narrator's moralistic interpretation continue, as the images of more streets, neighborhoods, and qualities are called
forth. The structure of the description, which seems to be
based upon radical contrast ("rues assassines" ["murderous
streets"], "rues estimables" ["respectable streets"], "rues toujours
propres, rues toujours sales" ["streets which are always clean;
streets which are always dirty"]), allows Balzac a considerable
freedom of movement. It allows him in fact to cover a terri-

tory larger than what the eye of the narrator could grasp, and it necessarily engages us in the activity of somehow linking the streets of Paris. The interpretation that the narrator imposes encourages us to formulate a moral and emotional image of the whole rather than one based on the physical unity that the streets imply. Because the description is composed more of the narrator's interpretation than it is of the actual naming of the streets, the former has more power over our reception of the passage. That interpretation depends heavily upon a highly charged and suggestive vocabulary; for example, "La place de la Bourse est babillarde, active, prostituée; elle n'est pas belle que par un clair de lune, à deux heures du matin: le jour, c'est un abrégé de Paris; pendant la nuit, c'est comme une rêverie de la Grèce" (5:793) ("Stock Exchange Square is all rattle, bustle and harlotry. It is beautiful only in the moonlight, at two in the morning; in the day-time an epitome of Paris, at night-time a dream-vision from Greece," p. 31). Like the city streets and the adjectives, interpretations themselves pile one atop the other to overwhelm the reader with the messages of movement, force, and invisible meaning.

Although the organization of the description seems based on a somewhat frenzied flight through the city of Paris, the passage is, in fact, highly structured in its relation to the reader. While the opening sentence thrusts us into the movement of it all, in the second sentence, the narrator tells us exactly what is his approach and what should be our stance vis-à-vis his evocation of the city: "Enfin, les rues de Paris ont des qualités humaines, et nous impriment par leur physionomie certaines idées contre lesquelles nous sommes sans défense" (5:793) ("In short, the streets of Paris have human qualities and such a physiognomy as leaves us with impressions against which we can put up no resistance," p. 31). As in the realistic description, the narrator dominates the scene and imposes a specific pattern of interpretation, yet he is portrayed as defenseless in the face of the exterior reality, which has inscribed certain ideas in his imagination, as unable to resist the meaning, the truth, that the streets inevitably yield. This truth, which is the essential abstracted meaning, is what the narrator will recount to us, and he implies that we too will be defenseless in the face of his narration. His abstract description will capture the dynamism of the scene, permitting him to wield power over us just as the scene did over him. The abstract description is an attempt, then, to reproduce the spell of the streets, and the narrator directs us, therefore, to allow ourselves to be put under that spell: "Si vous vous promenez dans les rues de l'île Saint-Louis, ne demandez raison de la tristesse nerveuse qui s'empare de vous qu'à la solitude, à l'air morne des maisons et des grands hôtels déserts" (5:793) ("If you wander along the streets of the Ile Saint-Louis, look for no other cause of the uneasy sadness that takes possession of you than the solitariness, the dejected appearance of its houses and forsaken mansions," p. 31). Furthermore, he anticipates our agreement: "La rue Traversière-Saint-Honoré n'est-elle pas une rue infâme?" (5:793) ("Is not the Rue Traversière-Saint-Honoré a street of ill fame . . . ?" p. 31). In other words, the description of the city becomes an exercise in "all-powerfulness," evoking by its dynamics the nature of the tale to be told. As the narrator imposes his interpretation upon us, we experience the kind of relationship that will be elaborated in *Ferragus*. Before we ever encounter the "Société des Treize," the setting of the scene prepares our understanding of it, because the narrator establishes within us a feeling for the city in terms of its atmosphere rather than its appearance.

In the abstract description, the domination of the narrator is effected, perhaps principally by the rapid movement of the focus of his description, which reduces the number of details included and thus leaves us little option but to accept his interpretation. From the street, his glance soars to the "méchantes petites maisons" (5:793) ("shabby houses," p. 31) that contain nothing but "des vices, des crimes, de la misère" (5:794) ("vice, crime and poverty," p. 31–32) and reverts quickly to the "rues étroites exposées au nord, où le soleil ne vient que trois ou quatre fois dans l'année" (5:794) ("narrow streets facing north which only enjoy a touch of sunlight three or four times a year," p. 32). From the present—"la Justice d'aujourd'hui ne s'en mêle pas" (5:794) ("justice today fights shy of them," p. 32)—he flies to the past—"mais autrefois le Parlement . . . aurait au moins rendu quelque arrêt contre la rue" (5:794) ("though in the old days perhaps the *Parlement* . . . at least would have delivered formal judgement against the street," p. 31). Lest we fall behind, the narrator summarizes: "Pour résumer ces idées par un example" (5:794) ("We can sum all this up in one example," p. 32). Finally, he offers one final succession of juxtapositions as if to clinch our impression of chaos, claiming that they are merely observations, and therefore founded in the real, and that we must be in Paris to understand them, thus returning us to our original point of departure, to the "senteur parisienne" ("Parisian flavour") of his stories, and to the persistent domination of the narrator:

> Ces observations, incompréhensibles au-delà de Paris, seront sans doute saisies par ces hommes d'étude et de pensée, de poésie et de plaisir qui savent récolter, en flânant dans Paris, la masse de jouissances flottantes, à toute heure, entre ses murailles; par ceux pour lesquels Paris est le plus délicieux des monstres: là, jolie femme; plus loin, vieux et pauvre; ici, tout neuf comme la monnaie d'un nouveau règne; dans ce coin, élégant comme une femme à la mode. Monstre complet d'ailleurs! (5:794)[28]

> (These observations, which outside Paris would have no application, will no doubt be comprehensible to those men of thought and study, those poetic voluptuaries who, as they saunter through Paris, are adept at gathering a whole harvest of enjoyable experiences, one which undulates like a field of ripe corn within the city walls—and also to those for whom Paris is the most delightful of monsters: here a pretty woman, farther off a poverty-stricken old hag; here as freshly minted as the coin of a new reign, and in another corner of the town as elegant as a lady of fashion. A monster, certainly, from head to foot.) (p. 32)

From its frenetic presentation of Parisian streets, the description is suddenly pulled together into the romantic metaphor of the monster. Although this was not an original metaphor but one common to the Romantics, its place within the description remains significant because it organizes both the narrator's portrayal and the reader's impression into images of power and infantile fantasy of force and, perhaps, of evil. It imposes an organization and lends even more life to the already dynamic description.

Ses greniers, espèce de tête pleine de science et de génie; ses premiers étages, estomacs heureux; ses boutiques, véritables pieds; de là partent tous les trotteurs, tous les affairés. Eh! quelle vie toujours active a le monstre? A peine le dernier frétillement des dernières voitures de bal cesse-t-il au coeur que déjà ses bras se remuent aux Barrières, et il se secoue lentement. Toutes les portes bâillent, tournent sur leurs gonds, comme les membranes d'un grand homárd, invisiblement manoeuvrées par trente mille hommes ou femmes, dont chacune ou chacun vit dans six pieds carrés, y possède une cuisine, un atelier, un lit, des enfants, un jardin, n'y voit pas clair, et doit tout voir. Insensiblement les articulations craquent, le mouvement se communique, la rue parle. A midi, tout est vivant, les cheminées fument, le monstre mange; puis il rugit, puis ses mille pattes s'agitent. Beau spectacle! Mais, ô Paris! qui n'a pas admiré tes sombres paysages, tes échappées de lumière, tes culs-de-sac profonds et silencieux; qui n'a pas entendu tes murmures, entre minuit et deux heures du matin, ne connaît encore rien de ta vraie poésie, ni de tes bizarres et larges contrastes. (5:794–95)

(Its head is in the garrets, inhabited by men of science and genius; the first floors house the well-filled stomachs; on the ground floor are the shops, the legs and feet, since the busy trot of trade goes in and out of them. And what an ever-bustling life this monster leads. Scarcely has the last distant rattle of carriages from the ballrooms died down in the centre before its arms are already stirring on the outer reaches and slowly awaking from torpor. Every door yawns open and turns on its hinges like the articulations of a huge lobster, invisibly operated by thirty thousand men or women, every one of whom occupies a space of six square feet per person, with a kitchen, a workshop, a bed, children and a garden; he or she can see but dimly in it and yet has to see everything. Imperceptibly these joints begin to crack, movement is passed on from one to another, the streets become noisy with talk. By midday all is alive, the chimneys are smoking, the monster eats; then it roars and stirs its thousand legs. A wonderful sight! But, O Paris! He who has not admired your sombre landscapes, shot here and there with streams of light, and your deep, mute, blind alleys; he who has not listened to your murmurings between midnight and two in the morning, still knows nothing of the real poetry within you, or of the strange, broad contrasts you offer.) (pp. 32–33)

The expansive urban setting, called forth in the opening of the narration, is here mastered by the narrator, controlled for the reader to grasp, indicating that it has already been interpreted. Indeed, the creation of a metaphor is the only way to evoke the whole instead of just its parts, and the presence of the awed narrator, "sans défense," permits the creation of a metaphor so highly manipulative of our reception. Balzac presented a narrator swept up in his own narration, leaping to a new level of interpretation by abandoning what little referentiality existed in the description: "Beau spectacle! Mais, ô Paris!" (5:794) ("A wonderful sight! But, o Paris!" p. 33). Caught up as the narrator is in the spectacular image, the central metaphor engenders others as the description races forward. Paris as monster becomes (5:795) "cette monstrueuse merveille" ("monstrous miracle"), "la tête du monde" ("the world's thinking box"), "une créature" ("a sentient being," all English p. 33). Within the context of the metaphor, more examples of the monstrous nature of the city arise until the narrator returns to his original point of departure, Parisian streets:

> Oui donc, il est des rues, ou des fins de rue, il est certaines maisons, inconnues pour la plupart aux personnes du grand monde, dans lesquelles une femme appartenant à ce monde ne saurait aller sans faire penser d'elle les choses les plus cruellement blessantes. (5:795)

> (Here it is: there are streets or street ends, there are certain houses unknown to most people in polite society which a woman belonging to it cannot enter without the most cruelly hurtful things being thought about her.) (p. 34)

We might apply to Balzac's evocation of the city his own appreciation of Cooper's treatment of landscape: "C'est le paysage 'actif' saisi dans sa vie et son mouvement, personnage principal de l'intrigue, raison suffisante du roman"[29] ("This is an 'active' landscape, portrayed in all its life and movement, an important character in the story, reason alone for the novel"). Through the imposing presence of the narrator, the projection of the powerless reader, the use of highly charged vocabulary and of metaphor, and through Balzac's unique structure, the Parisian landscape of *Ferragus* comes alive in a particularly vibrant way. Although Balzac complained in this passage that in fact his tale may barely be understood, he did all possible in the context of his description to assure that his reader would understand the nature of the intrigue to follow. As a final, almost ironic note, he added to the end of this opening description, "et c'est grande pitié que de raconter une histoirc à un public qui n'en épouse pas tout le mérite locale" (5:796) ("One is loath to tell a story to a public for whom local colour is a closed book," p. 34).

The description of the city in *Ferragus* demonstrates the way Balzac used an abstract description to manipulate his readers into and within his text. Presented the grand and evocative metaphor and a dominating narrator, the responsive reader is manipulated into feeling rather than visualizing that which is described. The highly evocative nature of the abstract description permitted Balzac to recall the impression it first creates; the image of the monstrous city recurs in the narration, for continued commentary upon events that take place within the scenes described.[30] The sense of the dynamic setting created in the opening description becomes an integral part of our understanding of the story, and thus it contributes to the illusion of reality that surrounds it. By reducing the dynamic forces of Paris to the rapid, almost frenetic, movement of the description and by abstracting its image through the interpretive metaphor of Paris as monster, Balzac effectively concentrated the enormous space and life of the city into the description. Unlike the objectivity, the distancing, in *La Recherche de l'absolu*, in *Ferragus* we are subjected to the force beneath the surface of that which is described. We are prepared for the narrative events to come—not by the lessons of the narrator on how to respond to them but by the experience of power and domination that the reading of the opening description imposes.

In *La Recherche de l'absolu*, Balzac ascribed a role to the description both in relation to the narration and to the activities that we carry out as recipients of the narration. In his view of society, milieu and event were inseparable, so it is not surprising that the description of milieu should be an important ingredient in the narration of events. In both novels considered here, the opening description serves to usher us into the narration, to introduce us to its dynamic as well as to the nature of our participation in it, and to encourage the establishment of an illusion of reality that will permeate our reading. However, whereas the function of the description remains constant, the techniques upon which each is based differ. The intellectual approach of the realistic description, fostered by the objective narrator who demonstrates each activity in which the reader is to be engaged, permits a careful and elaborate delineation of the relationship between cadre and event, description and narration, upon which the reader can draw in subsequent reading. The emotional appeal of the abstract description, on the other hand, founded in a single, unifying metaphor and in the rapid movement and interpretation of the narrator, thrusts the reader immediately into an atmosphere, the experience of which is essential to the grasp of the dynamics and power of the story. In both novels, it is clear that the opening description is a training ground for us as readers. Into both the realistic and the abstract descriptions, Balzac has encoded for us not only the organization of his narration but also the guidelines for our interpretation of it.

IV

MISE EN ABIME:
THE STRUCTURE OF THE SHORT STORY

"Fiction is transmissible,
and its transmission takes a toll."

Peter Brooks, *The
Melodramatic Imagination*

Pierre Laubriet has claimed that Balzac's artistry is most evident in his short stories, because the form demanded more from him than did others, because it concentrated within itself the major characteristics of the other forms, and because it obeyed the laws of the novel, adding a new and significant ingredient in its use of the marvelous.[1] Within the context of my study, the short story serves as an excellent vehicle for examining the relationship between narrative structure and the reception of the text. The nature of the short story, with its many restrictions, makes the structure perhaps its most significant element in relation to the reader.

Through structure, an author can most assuredly position the reader in relation to the text, within or outside the narration, restricting our movement or directing it by dictating to us our interpretive possibilities. We find in structure the grand strategy for controlling reception of the text, the grand strategy that contains the others that I am considering. Structure provides authors with one means of reducing the distance between themselves and their readers and can minimize the difficulties posed by the absence of the reader.[2]

In the short story, the primary restriction of length limits the functioning of all narrative elements. It is then logical to assume that great care must be taken in the development of each narrative element, in particular structure, the framework within which other textual strategies operate. Moreover, structure itself plays an important role in the dynamics of the narration. I maintain that the structure of a short story has more potential than any other narrative element for a complex and intricate manipulation of the reception of the text. Indeed, the carefully designed structure serves well the goals of clarity and simplicity that are of the essence in this form. Thus, using one of Balzac's well-known stories, we can examine the function of structure as it relates to the reception of the text, its dynamic vis-à-vis the reader, and the author's use of a complex design to guide us.

In "La Grande Bretèche," the structure of the narration assigns to us a specific position within the audience represented in the narration itself, as well as a particular role in the fundamental dynamic of the text. Balzac has projected between himself and his reader several other readers who form links in a chain connecting the author to us through his text. The complicated structure of the tale constructs an axis, at the poles of which are narrator and narrataire, speaker and listener, performer and audience, and, by extension, Balzac and his reader. The fundamental association of sender and receiver is mirrored on several levels within the narration, creating a *mise en abîme*, representation within a representation, of transformed images of the relationship (storyteller to audience) that links us to the author himself. This multiplication of the axis, which is the essence of narrative dynamics, necessarily draws us into the story, linking the fictional and the nonfictional recipients of the tale, blending reality and fiction. The structure of the narration then reduces the distance between the actual and the projected reader, fostering our active participation in the coproduction of "La Grande Bretèche." It engages us in the narrative process itself and, in so doing, enhances the impact of the total narration upon us. Thus, the structure upon which this short story rests permitted Balzac to generate with his reader an *abîme* of relationships that parallel the essential relationship established upon our reception of the tale.

Diana Festa McCormick claimed that Balzac was "un très

grand auteur de nouvelles, le plus varié et le plus original en francais"[3] ("a very great short story writer, the most varied and the most original in French"). She stated that the goal of the short story writer was to work through the form's many restrictions in order to capture and fascinate the audience, to suggest rather than to say. "La Grande Bretèche" not only does what she has suggested but also represents the actual process of enchantment and engagement. The tale becomes both a successful short story and a commentary on its own effect, process, creation, and reception. Although "La Grande Bretèche" shares its fundamental structure (based on the manipulation of the framed tale and on the *mise en abîme*) with numerous other short stories, it is perhaps an extreme example, one more highly complicated than the others and clearer in its manipulation of the reader, especially as it indulges us in our search for literary pleasure. Inscribed in every level of the narration is the specific goal of audience entertainment, and it is that goal, pleasure, that directs the story toward its recipients and that focuses the narration upon its own reception. The pleasure that is ours is the pleasure of the charmed listener, the enchanted recipient of the tale. Thus, each of the three smaller narrations within the story, and the larger one of "La Grande Bretèche" itself, becomes an object of value. Indeed, the very process of narration, even more than the event being narrated, is the heart of the story.

The structure of "La Grande Bretèche" is rendered even more interesting by its placement as the final narration of four assembled under the title of *Autre Etude de femme*. Nicole Mozet has called this collection a puzzle made of pieces of diverse origin (3:657).[4] That it is tied to three other narrations within the context of *Autre Etude de femme* (after dinner storytelling) squarely places "La Grande Bretèche" in the milieu of entertainment, specifically, entertainment of an audience represented within the narration itself. Its placement in *Autre Etude de femme* makes "La Grande Bretèche" itself a puzzle, just one piece of a larger configuration. The most significant advantage to this positioning, however, is that it permits the actual representation of the audience, whose enthusiasm gives us a formal point of entry into the narration, an easily assumed position, and a clearly defined role. Furthermore, it puts us squarely in the presence of the narrator (one of the dinner guests), whose task it is to entertain us. By suggestion, at least, we will be as susceptible as the other members of the audience to the narrator's charm. Although we are initially outside "La Grande Bretèche" (its structure will reduce that distance), we are most clearly within the larger narration because we are fictionally represented there. As we take our place as members of the audience, we complete the axis narrator-narrataire; we are the audience for whom the narration is designed.

The context of the dinner party places us as well within an atmosphere of congeniality, relaxation, and enthusiasm. Not content simply to suggest that atmosphere, Balzac had his narrator stress it, explaining that it is the second and the better half of the evening, when only "quelques artistes, des gens gais, des amis" ("a few artists, high-spirited people, friends") remain: "la seconde, la véritable soirée . . . où l'on est forcé d'avoir de l'esprit et de contribuer à l'amusement public" (3:673) ("the second, the true evening. . . where one is obliged to have wit and to contribute to the general amusement"). The narrator clearly announces what the structure will reveal: the audience is of extreme importance to this narration, to its completion and interpretation, and to the forces that will permit it to function.

> Le souvenir d'une de ces soirées m'est plus particulièrement resté, moins à cause d'une confidence où l'illustre de Marsay mit à découvert un des replis les plus profonds du coeur de la femme, qu'à cause des observations auxquelles son récit donna lieu sur les changements qui se sont opérés chez la femme française depuis la fatale révolution de Juillet. (3:674)

> (The memory of one of these soirées has particularly remained with me, less because of a confidence in which the illustrious De Marsay opened one of the most profound depths of the feminine heart, than because of the observations to which his recital gave rise on the changes that have taken place in the French woman since the fatal July revolution.)

To entice us even further into the narrations to come and into our role within their production, the narrator adds, "Jamais le phénomène oral qui, bien étudié, bien manié, fait la puissance de l'acteur et du conteur, ne m'avait si complètement ensorcelé" (3:675) ("Never had oral performance, which when well studied and handled is the strength of the actor and the storyteller, so completely bewitched me"). As a final gesture of assurance, one that particularly emphasizes the goal of entertainment and the enthusiasm of the group, the narrator ends his preparatory remarks:

> Est-il besoin de dire qu'il n'y avait plus de domestiques, que les portes étaient closes et les portières tirées? Le silence fut si profond qu'on entendit dans la cour le murmure des cochers, les coups de pied et les bruits que font les chevaux en demandant à revenir à l'écurie. (3:677)

> (It is necessary to say that there were no longer any servants present, that the doors had been closed and the curtains drawn? The silence was so complete that one could hear the sounds of the coachmen in the courtyard, the sounds of the horses' hooves and the noises that they make when they want to return to the stable.)

Thus, the narrator sets the stage for the four tales to come, encouraging us to see ourselves as part of the group of listeners, a group that he describes as consisting of the brightest personalities, the most sophisticated wits, and the best of friends.

The atmosphere created in the opening is maintained and enhanced throughout the recitation of the first three tales, which build up to the opening of "La Grande Bretèche." This last of the four narrations is introduced in a manner appropriate to the structure upon which it is built and to the dynamic that will propel it. It also introduces the singular element that serves as the catalyst for each internal narration within "La Grande Bretèche" as well as for the whole, that is, the desire of the recipient to hear another tale, the curiosity of the listener that entices the narrator to go on. The movement of "La Grande Bretèche" hinges upon the desire of the recipients represented in the text, and the structure depends on this element for its effectiveness. The transition then from the third narration in *Autre Etude de femme* to the fourth, "La Grande Bretèche," is the expression of desire from the audience, and it establishes the axis between narrator and narrataire as well as the significance of audience approval and pleasure.

> — Les histoires que conte le docteur, dit le duc de Rhétoré, font des impressions bien profondes.
> — Mais douces, reprit Mlle des Touches.
> — Ah! madame, répliqua le docteur, j'ai des histoires terribles dans mon répertoire; mais chaque récit a son heure dans une conversation. . . .
> — Mais il est deux heures du matin, et l'histoire de Rosine nous a préparées, dit la maîtresse de la maison.
> — Dites, monsieur Bianchon! . . . demanda-t-on de tous côtés. (3:710)

> ("The stories that the doctor tells," said the Duc de Rhétoré," leave very profound impressions."
> "But gentle ones," replied Mlle des Touches.
> "Ah! madame," the doctor answered, "I have terrible stories in my repertoire; but every telling has its own hours in a conversation....
> "But it is two o'clock in the morning, and the story of Rosina has prepared us," said the mistress of the house.
> "Go ahead, Monsieur Bianchon! . . ." was uttered from every side.)

One might well apply to "La Grande Bretèche" the description of structure that Nicole Mozet offered for *Autre Etude de femme*, "une vertigineuse construction en abîme" (3:664) ("a dizzying and cavernous construction"). The structure of "La Grande Bretèche" creates the relationship that propels the entire narration, creates the very relationship that allows it to exist as structure. Not only does it establish the axis between storyteller and audience, but it multiplies and mirrors it at every level of the narration. Through this mirrorlike representation of the context and essence of narration, of the basic relationship between Balzac and his reader, every detail of the narration is placed within the framework that maintains contact with and entertains the active and subjective reader. The cause-and-effect relationship that functions along this axis is reciprocal: impact of the narration shapes audience response, which in turn shapes the form and the art of storytelling. The cause-and-effect relationship, so basic to all literature, is duplicated and transformed throughout "La Grande Bretèche" as the narrator, Bianchon, becomes the recipient of the tale and as former recipients step forward to narrate portions of it.

"La Grande Bretèche" contains three separate blocks of narration, each with its own narrator. Although each block relates to the central event of the story, each one pertains to a period different from the others (before, during, and after the central event). Because the individual blocks of narration give us new information to be integrated into the whole of our perception, we are moved closer to the central event. From another point of view, however, one could say that the block structure removes us by several degrees from the event itself. All three narrators have been recipients of their narrations and within "La Grande Bretèche" relate their tales to Bianchon, who, in turn, tells them at the dinner party. At least four receptions of the tale or bits of it precede ours, and the last two of those are represented within the narration itself. Thus, each block of narration revolves around an axis like the fundamental one of the text, linking narrator and narrataire, creating the *mise en abîme* upon which this structure rests and activating its dynamic cycle of desire and narration. Rather than the horrible story of Mme de Merret, the recitation and reception of the tale stand before us and compose, essentially, the theme of "La Grande Bretèche": as each block engenders the next, using as sole transition the response of the narrator-turned-narrataire, Bianchon, we become part of the dynamic in which the curiosity of the audience engenders a narration, which evokes a response from the audience, which leads to another narration, until the process is abruptly brought to an end. The focus of the tale thus falls squarely on the acts of narration and reception and on the transaction between audience and narrator. Thus, although we are separated by so many recipients from the event being narrated, we are not separated from the narration of "La Grande Bretèche" itself because our position and our function are so clearly framed within.

Bianchon's presentation of "La Grande Bretèche" opens with a description of the old house and the property that gives its name to the short story. The estate is portrayed mysteriously, its ruinous condition being the result of some unknown and probably awful event. Moreover, the opening description, mirroring the pattern of *Autre Etude de femme,* is put into a context of entertainment: Bianchon visited the abandoned property for the pleasurable effect it had upon him and upon his imagination. In fact, the pleasure kept him from wanting to know the truth about the old house, for fear that it would be less interesting than his own fabrications. But the very fact that the property arouses his curiosity or a desire for a narration (his own more than what he receives) is enough to engender the first block of narration, from which he and we find the first of the essential facts of the tale.

The opening description, however, is not merely a pretense to usher in the first of the supplementary narrators. It sets the tone for the narration to come. It combines realistic and abstract description as it alternately focuses our attention on the narration itself and on the narrator. The description is realistic enough in detail—"Quelques saules, nés dans le Loir, ont rapidement poussé comme la haie de clôture et cachent à demi la maison" (3:710) ("Willows with their roots in the Loir have grown quickly, like the boundary hedge, and half conceal the house," p. 176)—but the narrator interprets and transforms each detail to indicate its effect upon him and the questioning that it provoked, passing on to us a sense of the Gothic atmosphere that enshrouded the property: "D'énormes lézardes sillonnent les murs, dont les crètes noircies sont enlacées par les mille festons de la pariétaire" (3:711) ("Enormous cracks furrow the walls, whose blackened tops are festooned by a thousand garlands of pellitory," p. 177). Clearly, the description of milieu points to a grand cause and is designed to evoke in us the desire for search (to be fulfilled by the narration): "Une invisible main a partout écrit le mot: MYSTÈRE!" (3:711) ("Everywhere an invisible hand has written the word MYSTERY," p. 177). The description focuses our attention not only upon the deserted property but also upon the narrator in the midst of all that he describes. Even as the house is represented as the effect of some terrible cause, it becomes the cause of a significant effect upon the narrator: "Quel feu tombé du ciel a passé par là? Quel tribunal a ordonné de semer du sel sur ce logis? —Y a-t-on insulté

Dieu? Y a-t-on trahi la France? Voilà ce qu'on se demande"
(3:711) ("What fire from heaven has fallen this way? What
court of law has given the order to scatter salt on this dwelling? Has God been insulted here? Has France been betrayed
here? These are the questions you ask yourself," p. 177). The
narrator concludes his impression of the property with the
only interpretation possible: "Cette maison, vide et déserte,
est une immense énigme dont le mot n'est connu de personne"
(3:711) ("The empty deserted house is an immense riddle to
which no one knows the answer," p. 177). The key to the
enigma will be contained only in the narration, which then
becomes a necessity. Thus, the description represents the
process by which we are to be drawn into the narration as well
as our function within it. We must allow ourselves to be
seized by the narration as Bianchon was by the sight of the
property. We must question both cause and effect, allowing
our curiosity and imagination to be aroused. We will then, as
he did, take delight in the exchange.

> Là, je composais de délicieux romans; je m'y livrais à de petites
> débauches de mélancolie qui me ravissaient. Si j'avais connu le
> motif, peut-être vulgaire, de cet abandon, j'eusse perdu les po-
> ésies inédites dont je m'enivrais. Pour moi cet asile representait
> les images les plus variées de la vie humaine, assombrie par ses
> malheurs: c'était tantôt l'air du cloître, moins les religieux; tantôt
> la paix du cimetière, sans les morts qui vous parlent leur langage
> épitaphique; aujourd'hui la maison du lépreux, demain celle
> des Atrides; mais c'était surtout la province avec ses idées re-
> cueillies, avec sa vie de sablier. J'y ai souvent pleuré, je n'y ai
> jamais ri. Plus d'une fois j'ai ressenti des terreurs involontaires en
> y entendant, au-dessus de ma tête, le sifflement sourd que rendaient
> les ailes de quelque ramier pressé. (3:712)

(There, I made up delightful stories, I succumbed to charming
little orgies of melancholy. If I had known the reason, perhaps very
ordinary, for this desertion I would have lost the unpublished
fictions with which I intoxicated myself. For me, this refuge
represented the most varied images of human life, clouded by
misfortunes. At times it had the atmosphere of a monastery without the monks, at times the peace of the cemetery without the
dead who speak in their epitaphs. Today it is a leper house, tomor-
row it will be the house of the Atridae. But, above all, it was
provincial life with its meditations and its slow tempo. I have
often wept there, I have never laughed there. More than once I

have felt involuntary terror as I heard over my head the dull whirring of the wings of some hastening wood-pigeon.) (p. 178)

The focus on the narrator in relation to the object described is significant for another reason as well. Bianchon's response to the sight is one of imagination and sensitivity, his description delicately drawn. Thus, the narrator is established as a talented one, a narrator from whom we can anticipate an entertaining and sensitive narration.[5] Furthermore, he is represented here as a recipient (not yet of the narrations, but at least of the impact of the scene), and so our identification with him in that role begins.

We then move to the first block of narration and to a new narrator, M. Regnault. In general terms, the change of narrator focuses our attention once again on the narrative process, adding a certain intensity and vivacity to the storytelling. Moreover, it keeps us just the slightest bit off balance as Bianchon relinquishes in part his role as narrator to assume ours as narrataire. Bianchon retains the floor long enough, however, to offer us a caricature of the next narrator, a humorous portrayal of M. Regnault's appearance and dress that draws a sharp contrast to the seriousness of the opening description, its somber mood, and the excitement that its mystery stirred:

> Tout à coup je vis apparaître un homme long, fluet, vêtu de noir, tenant son chapeau à la main, et qui se présenta comme un bélier prêt à fondre sur son rival, en me montrant un front fuyant, une petite tête pointue et une face pâle, assez semblable à un verre d'eau sale. . . . Cet inconnu portait un vieil habit, très usé sur les plis; mais il avait un diamant au jabot de sa chemise et des boucles d'or à ses oreilles. (3:713)

> (Suddenly there came in a tall, spare man dressed in black, holding his hat in his hand, who introduced himself like a ram ready to butt his rival. He had a receding brow, a little pointed head and a pale face rather like a glass of dirty water. . . . This stranger was wearing an old jacket very worn at the seams. But he had a diamond on his shirt ruff and gold rings in his ears.) (pp. 178–79)

The caricature specifically draws our attention away from the deserted property and focuses it upon this character and even more directly upon the act of narration and the goal of entertainment. Even while it stalls the delivery of M. Regnault's narration, the caricature draws us into the text, enticing us with the curious question of what relationship could possibly exist between this character and the abandoned property. It arouses our curiosity, our desire for the next narration. Even as M. Regnault begins that narration, we are engaged in the appropriate search for clues about the truth of the old house, and we learn that many before us have sought these clues— "monsieur, je n'en finirais pas si je vous répétais tous les contes qui se sont débités à [l'égard de Mme de Merret]" (3:715) ("Monsieur, I would never finish if I were to repeat to you all the stories which have been told about [Mme de Merret]," p. 181).

The narration, however, offers only a few facts regarding the property: Mme de Merret, its owner, ordained in her last testament that the property not be entered or altered in any way until fifty years after her death; M. de Merret died alone in Paris, worn out by debauchery; Mme de Merret died a horrible death to which Regnault was a witness, after she had already abandoned the property in question. Bianchon's curiosity is aroused by the tale—despite a preference for his own romanticized versions of the story behind "La Grande Bretèche." "Il me fallait dire adieu à mes belles rêveries, à mes romans; je ne fus donc pas rebelle au plaisir d'apprendre la vérité d'une manière officielle" (3:714) ("I had to bid farewell to my beautiful daydreams, to my romances. So I had no objection to the pleasure of learning the truth officially," p. 180).

We witness then another scene in which Bianchon, the narrator-narrataire, is himself drawn into this narration. It is the narration itself, the "manière officielle," that pleases him more than the truth. Regnault's narration builds to a high point in the description of the death of Mme de Merret. Its intensity and its evocative language return us to the Gothic atmosphere alluded to at the opening of the short story. Regnault himself, however, places the scene squarely in the context of storytelling: "Ah! mon cher monsieur, si vous aviez vu, comme je la vis alors, cette vaste chambre tendue en tapisseries brunes, vous vous seriez cru transporté dans une véritable scène de roman" (3:716) ("Oh, my dear sir, if you had seen, as I did then, that enormous room draped with brown tapestries, you would have thought you had been transported into a veritable scene from a novel," p. 182). Indeed, storytelling is of the essence; when Regnault's narration becomes too confusing and boring or when it is delivered in a monotone, Bianchon steps in to take over again as narrator. Bianchon tells us Regnault's "observations étaient si contradictoires, si diffuses, que je faillis m'endormir, malgré l'intérêt que je prenais à cette histoire authentique" (3:718) ("observations were so contradictory and so diffuse, that I almost fell asleep in spite of the interest which I took in this true story," p. 184). Only the well-told tale is worth the telling.

Even within this first block of narration, the internal cause-and-effect relationships are being altered, crossed, and transformed. The property is the effect of some terrible cause. It, in turn, causes Bianchon's curiosity to be aroused. That curiosity leads inevitably to M. Regnault's narration, spurring Bianchon to seek more information about the house and its story. But Regnault's narration is of the effect; he does not know the cause of Mme de Merret's actions, the terrible event behind the abandonment of the house. On the level of the short story itself, we are moving ever so slowly in the reverse direction of the mystery, from effect to cause. Structurally, however, the direction is clearly the contrary, from cause to effect, from desire to narration. At the time of Regnault's story, the relationship between the event narrated and its narration is singularly different from that established between the narration and its recipients. Nevertheless, as recipients we participate in both, which permits us to anticipate and to seek out the next block of narration, simultaneously questioning it in both a forward and a backward movement in an effort to relate cause and effect definitively.

The independent blocks of narration are joined by the observation, reactions, and reflections of Bianchon who reassumes his role as narrator. Each transition is tied to the opening of the story, reevoking the Gothic atmosphere of the property and focusing upon the imagination and sensitivity of Bianchon. The opening description, in conjunction with the transitions between blocks of narration, forms a context into which the facts of the tale are incorporated. It is a context that presents the act of reception, the search in progress, and the pleasure that they yield. Between the narration of M. Regnault and the one that follows, there is a short yet significant passage:

> je m'assis dans mon fauteuil, en mettant mes pieds sur les deux chenets de ma cheminée. Je m'enfonçais dans un roman à la Radcliffe, bâti sur les données juridiques de M. Regnault, quand ma porte, manoeuvrée par la main adroite d'une femme, tourna sur ses gonds. (3:718–19)

> (I sat down in my armchair, putting my feet on the two firedogs in my fireplace. I became absorbed in a Radcliffe-like novel, based on the legal information given by Monsieur Regnault, when my door, manipulated by a woman's light hand, turned on its hinges.) (pp. 184–85)

We discover here the reaction of Bianchon to Regnault's tale, and the questioning to which that reaction leads offers to the reader an example of appropriate participation, as Bianchon ties together the Gothic atmosphere of the opening and the newly discovered facts. He still has insufficient evidence to begin serious detective work, however. What is essential, though, is the example he sets as narrataire and the attendant possibility for reader identification with that role. We are represented in the text not only in the form of the audience to whom Bianchon recounts his tale, but in the character of Bianchon himself as he dons the recipient's role and then, as narrator, comments upon it, accelerating our interest in the unfolding story with his own and further demonstrating the significance of Bianchon's alternating roles vis-à-vis the reader. The process permits, even encourages, identification with Bianchon. Built into the text, then, is the mechanism by which we are able to place ourselves within the narration at various levels, perceiving the relationship of recipient to narration mirrored throughout and perceiving as well the desire-and-narration cycle.

Bianchon's desire, the effect of the first narration, becomes the catalyst for the second, that of the hotel keeper, Mère Lepas. Because her block of information involves a leap to a temporal plane anterior to that of Regnault's narration, she is able to offer the first bits of information about the reasons behind Mme de Merret's testament. With this block, the story takes a new turn and requires of us a greater degree of association, questioning, and guessing. As Mère Lepas presents more questions to be answered, our desire for a specific narration increases, for the narration that will unlock the mystery of the abandoned property. Bianchon clearly indicates his desire as he coaxes the hotel keeper to give him more information, applying pressure when she resists. "Ma chère dame Lepas! ajoutai-je en terminant, vous paraissez en savoir davantage. Hein? Autrement pourquoi seriez-vous montée chez moi? . . . vos yeux sont gros d'un secret. Vous avez connu M. de Merret. Quel homme était-ce?" (3:719) (" 'Madame Lepas, my good woman,' I added as I finished. 'You seem to know more about it, don't you? Otherwise, why did you come up to my room? . . . Your eyes are laden with a secret. You knew Monsieur de Merret. What kind of a man was he?' " p. 185). We learn from Mère Lepas the story of the Spaniard whom she suspects of a liaison with Mme de Merret. He returned late each night to the hotel but was once found swimming across the river from La Grande Bretèche, and, finally, he mysteriously disappeared some time before Mme de Merret abandoned her property. The puzzle begins to take some shape, and our hypothesizing (mirrored within by the Gothic romanticizing and the specific questioning of Bianchon) is given some direction. Mère Lepas offers us information to tie her narration with that of Regnault, information that points equally to the narration to come. (A central object in "La Grande Bretèche" is a crucifix that Regnault says Mme de Merret kissed as a final gesture before her death. Mère Lepas tells us that the Spaniard possessed one identical to it but no longer had it when he disappeared.) As we leap from after to before the central event, from the effect to the cause, the narration assumes a form for us that is not presented in the text itself. The narration of Mère Lepas is filled with signs to guide us, not the least of which is the final one, pointing us directly to the next narrator. When Bianchon asks Mère Lepas if she has not questioned Rosalie, who works for her but who worked previously for Mme de Merret, Mère

Lepas responds, "Cette fille-là, c'est un mur. Elle sait quelque chose; mais il est impossible de la faire jaser." (3:722) ("That girl, she's like a wall. She knows something but it's impossible to get her to spill the beans," p. 188). She thus closes her narration on a note of suspense but with a clear indication of the direction Bianchon is to take. On all levels of the narration, now, we are moving from cause to effect: one narrator points to another; one narration generates another; and we close in on the narration of the event at the heart of the tale.

The transition between this block of narration and the one to follow is more interesting and certainly more provocative than the first transition. Not content simply to recall the atmosphere of the opening description, Bianchon adds to it by creating new effects of mystery and the fantastic, enhancing the entertainment value of this block of narration by embellishing it.

Après avoir encore causé pendant un moment avec moi, mon hôtesse me laissa en proie à des pensées vagues et ténébreuses, à une curiosité romanesque, à une terreur religieuse assez semblable au sentiment profond qui nous saisit quand nous entrons à la nuit dans une église sombre où nous apercevons une faible lumière lointaine sous des arceaux élevés; une figure indécise glisse, un frottement de robe ou de soutane se fait entendre . . . nous avons frissonné. La Grande Bretèche et ses hautes herbes, ses fenêtres condamnées, ses ferrements rouillés, ses portes closes, ses appartements déserts, se montra tout à coup fantastiquement devant moi. J'essayai de pénétrer dans cette mystérieuse demeure en y cherchant le noeud de cette solennelle histoire, le drame qui avait tué trois personnes. (3:722)

(After chatting with me for a moment longer, my landlady left me a prey to vague, gloomy thoughts, to a romantic curiosity, to a religious terror rather like the deep feeling which grips us when, at night, we go into a dark church where we can see a faint, distant light under lofty arches; an indeterminate figure glides past, the rustle of a dress or a surplice can be heard . . . we have shuddered. La Grande Bretèche and its tall grasses, its condemned windows, its rusty ironwork, its closed doors, its deserted rooms, suddenly rose fantastically before me. I tried to penetrate the mystery of this dwelling as I searched for the clue of the solemn story, the drama that had killed three people.) (pp. 188–89)

Within this atmosphere, then, the imagination and the curiosity of Bianchon are aroused to such a degree that inevitably he seeks out the third narration. We witness the process shown in this transition, however, through the attention he has fixed on the next narrator, following the lead of Mère Lepas. Bianchon describes in such detail his concentration upon the new narrator that we as well are forced to focus our attention upon Rosalie, the key to the narration we seek. Indeed, Rosalie takes on a symbolic value vis-à-vis the story being narrated, because she alone knows the most significant portion of the tale. But she also bears symbolic value in relation to the structural dynamic that is so important to our reading. Clearly, hers is the final block. Her narration will bring us as close to the center as we are able to get, as close to the actual event as is possible. Thus, the narrator concentrates upon her and upon his own reaction to her. Still, as narrator, he anticipates his role as recipient of her narration. The more he dwells upon her (and, therefore, as we do), the more symbolic value she acquires as keeper of the narrative.

> Rosalie fut à mes yeux l'être le plus intéressant de Vendôme. Je découvris, en l'examinant, les traces d'une pensée intime, malgré la santé brillante qui éclatait sur son visage potelé. Il y avait chez elle un principe de remords ou d'espérance; son attitude annonçait un secret, comme celle des dévotes qui prient avec excès ou celle de la fille infanticide qui entend toujours le dernier cri de son enfant ... Rosalie me paraissait située dans cette histoire romanesque comme la case qui se trouve au milieu d'un damier; elle était au centre même de l'intérêt et de la vérité; elle me semblait nouée dans le noeud. Ce ne fut plus une séduction ordinaire à tenter, il y avait dans cette fille le dernier chapitre d'un roman; aussi, dès ce moment, Rosalie devint-elle l'objet de ma prédilection. (3:722–23)

> (In my eyes Rosalie was the most interesting person in Vendôme. On looking at her carefully, I discovered the traces of a secret thought, despite the glowing health which beamed from her plump face. She had within her a source of remorse or of hope. Her demeanour suggested that she had a secret, like that of pious women who pray excessively, or of a girl guilty of infanticide who always hears her child's last cry.... Rosalie seemed to me to have a place in this romantic story like the square in the middle of a chess-board. She was in the very centre of the interest and of the truth. She seemed to me to be tied up in the web. It wasn't an

ordinary seduction that I had to attempt. In this girl there was the last chapter of a novel. So, from that moment, Rosalie became the object of my predilection.) (pp. 189–90)

All that has come before in "La Grande Bretèche" acts upon Bianchon, once again narrataire, now that he is so near to receiving the final narration, indeed, "the last chapter of [his] novel," and to satisfying his desire. This is a high point of suspense in the narration for the narrator and audience alike. Bianchon coaxes Rosalie to relinquish her narration, just as, earlier, the audience had begged him to recount his tale. Bianchon underscores the importance of his desire for the narration and the way in which it serves as catalyst within the narrative process.

> [Rosalie] eut bientôt tous les attraits que notre désir prête aux femmes, dans quelque situation qu'elles puissent être. Quinze jours après la visite du notaire, un soir, ou plutôt un matin, car il était de très bonne heure, je dis à Rosalie: "Raconte-moi donc tout ce que tu sais sur Mme de Merret?" (3:723)

> (Soon [Rosalie] had all the attractions that our desire lends to women in whatever situation they may be. A fortnight after the lawyer's visit, one evening, or rather, one morning, for it was very early, I said to Rosalie, "Tell me everything you know about Madame de Merret.") (p. 190)

Bianchon brings us to the edge of the desired narration (after considerable stalling), but he abruptly substitutes himself for Rosalie as narrator, emphasizing once again the goal of entertainment and the proposition that a tale is not worth telling unless it is well told. He abbreviates what she has told him, explaining the event that led to the abandonment of the property, the first two narrations, and, indirectly, his own search. On a structural level, all that has come before has pointed us to this narration, prepared us for it, and made us await it with little patience. Rosalie's story is the effect of all that has preceded it in the text; it is the structural completion or conclusion. On the narrative level, however, it is the cause and not the effect of all that precedes it in the narration.

As Bianchon introduces the final block of narration, he signals to us yet another leap in time, reinforcing the concept of countermovements of cause and effect within the structure of the story. The opposite movements of the tale itself and of its reading converge in the final narration, for which we have been so fully prepared that only a few words need be spoken.

> Or, comme l'événement dont [Rosalie] me donna la confuse connaissance se trouve placé entre le bavardage du notaire et celui de Mme Lepas, aussi exactement que les moyens termes d'un proportion arithmétique le sont entre leurs deux extrêmes, je n'ai plus qu'à vous le dire en peu de mots. J'abrège donc. (3:724)

> (Now, since the event of which [Rosalie] gave me a jumbled account is situated between the lawyer's and Madame Lepas' gossip as exactly as the middle terms of an arithmetical progression are between their two extremes, it only remains for me to tell it to you in a few words. So I abbreviate.) (p. 190)

In the third block of narration, then, Bianchon supplies only the barest details, with neither interpretation nor association with former passages. Nothing impedes the swift delivery of the story. Speaking in a considerably accelerated rhythm, Bianchon races to the climax of the tale with none of his former romanticizing. In this part of the short story, he is a pure narrator, no longer a narrataire. We therefore learn quickly the story at the heart of "La Grande Bretèche": how M. de Merret walled his wife's lover, the Spaniard, into a closet even as he forced her to swear upon her crucifix that there was no one inside and how he remained with her in the room for twenty days as the Spaniard died. The end of the tale forces us to reconsider each detail of the preceding narrations: her terrible death, his in Paris, the state of the house, her last testament, the Spaniard in the river, the crucifix, and so on. Once we have received the final narration, details fall into their proper order, leaving us the task of rearranging all that we have learned, a process that is not part of our actual reading but one that follows the reading once the narrator has given us our leave.

The final passage of "La Grande Bretèche" (at which point we are released) presents the reaction of the audience to Bianchon's narration, thrusting us suddenly back to the outer layer of the structure. That is, we return to the narrator-audience axis exterior to the narration of "La Grande Bretèche" but interior to that of the collection, *Autre Etude de femme.* The conclusion completes the transaction that has, by the mirroring of the narrator-narrataire axis and the block structure, guided us to the center of the *abîme* and out again.

> Après ce récit, toutes les femmes se levèrent de table, et le charme sous lequel Bianchon les avait tenues fut dissipé par ce mouvement. Néanmoins quelques-unes d'entre elles avaient eu quasi froid en entendant le dernier mot. (3:729)

> (After this story, all the women rose from the table, and the charm under which Bianchon had held them was dissipated by this movement. Nevertheless, some among them had had something like a chill on hearing the last word.)

The dispersal of the group signals the end of its desire for further narration, and, thus, *Autre Etude de femme* comes to a close. The cycle of desire-narration has been broken. The concluding passage represents a second denouement to the action that interrupts and therefore destroys the axis between narrator and narrataire. The representation of the effect of the narration at this level is certainly parallel to the frequent representation of Bianchon's reaction to the various narrations within "La Grande Bretèche." It invites us to consider our own reaction and the axis that exists between us as readers and Balzac as raconteur. The response of the audience is important commentary on storytelling; even among Bianchon's highly sophisticated audience, the well-told tale has its magic power.[6] So when we step back and rearrange the pieces, we realize that the response of the recipient—Bianchon, his audience, and ourselves—remains in large measure the focus of the short story.

Clearly, a mystery story like "La Grande Bretèche," a tale for which the impact of the final scenes is of the greatest importance, relies on two facts: our reading follows a certain order; through that ordered reading, information can be withheld or given so as to maximize the impact of the ending when all falls into place. The structure of "La Grande Bretèche" is the single most significant element in the control of its reading and in the preparation of the reader for the impact of the ending. It is largely because of the tale's complicated structure that we are kept off balance, that the all-important desire for narration is kept alive, that the tone is varied and roles exchanged, and, finally, that we can function on various temporal levels at once. More than simply controlling our interpretation, structure manipulates us into a position vis-à-vis the narration itself so that all the other narrative elements enjoy their fullest role in relation to the reader. In "La Grande Bretèche," it is the structure that permits us to see ourselves reflected within the narration and that permits us to become in part its subject. Furthermore, it is the structure that induces us to contemplate the relationship between author and reader. The complexity of the structure and the complicity that its dynamic requires of us, then, together serve the text's stated goal, entertainment.

V

MASTERY OF *LA COMEDIE HUMAINE:* THE REAPPEARING CHARACTER

Mais la victoire définitive de Balzac sur son
grande aîné, sa libération par rapport à lui,
s'exprime par une invention extraordinaire qui
va transformer entièrement la structure de son
oeuvre, lui permettant de faire du roman à la
Walter Scott un détail ou un chapitre de ce
qu'il considère, lui, comme son roman. Il s'agit
du retour des peronnages.

(But the definitive victory of Balzac over his
great elder, his liberation in relationship to
him, expresses itself by an extraordinary invention that was to transform the structure of his
work entirely, permitting him to make the novel
à la Walter Scott a detail or a chapter of what
he himself considered as his novel. I refer to
the reappearance of characters.)

Butor, "Balzac et la réalité"

The final strategy that I shall discuss, the reappearing character, represents a different approach on Balzac's part to the
problem of accommodation in the narration of an active
reader. Indeed, in the use of this technique, Balzac appears to
have relinquished much of his control in order to encourage
creativity and a more subjective contribution from the reader
to the shape of the character and, therefore, to the meaning of
the narration. According to Fernand Lotte, Balzac created 573
reappearing characters within his work.[1] Through them he
offers to us, his readers, the greatest challenge in our efforts to

master *La Comédie humaine* as well as one of the richest sources of reading pleasure.

Balzac claimed, by way of Félix Davin, "Il ne suffit pas d'être un homme, il faut être un système"[2] ("It is not enough to be a man, one must be a system"). Moreover, we know that is was of extreme importance to him that his work be unified, that it constitute not merely a series of vignettes but a monument to and of his day. The most significant source of unity in Balzac's monument—the fictional extension of his "système"—is its array of reappearing characters. This technique not only furnished him with a unifying principle but also offers the reader a network of relationships through which to unite the many separate stories and novels in which the characters appear, forming the fictional universe that is *La Comédie humaine*. The result, according to Butor, is "un mobile romanesque, un ensemble formé d'un certain nombre de parties que nous pouvons aborder presque dans l'ordre que nous désirons; chaque lecteur découpera dans l'univers de *La Comédie humaine* un trajet différent; c'est comme une sphère ou une enceinte avec de multiples portes"[3] ("a fictional mobile, a whole made up of a certain number of parts that we can tackle in almost any order we would like; every reader will cut a different path through the universe of *La Comédie humaine*; it is like a sphere or an enclosure with numerous doors"). Due in part to the unifying influence of the reappearing characters, our reading of an individual text or of the whole depends on a dynamic movement within the confines of the fictional universe. The demands made upon us for the mastery of the ensemble are of course different from and, in a sense, greater than those involved in the reading of an individual text. By the same token, the means of manipulating our response at the author's disposal are less concentrated, spanning as they do so many narrations. Because of the very breadth of his invention, Balzac has granted us greater interpretive freedom. The ultimate unification of his work requires the very creativity that the technique of the reappearing character fosters.

The reading process by which we actualize reappearing characters involves a nonlinear or synchronic reading. The nature of the technique, which draws otherwise unrelated texts together, permits us to perceive a character on several levels (that is, in several texts) at once. The more often we encounter a character in our reading, the more we must complicate that character's unfolding story and the more nonlinear our reading becomes, as the character then becomes more significant within each narration as well as within the broad narration, *La Comédie humaine*. Because the presence of the reappearing character places a given text in a permanent relationship with all others in which that character appears, each narration potentially bypasses its own limits. As we read it in the light of others we have encountered, it takes meaning from and adds meaning to them. The reappearance of a character is thus a provocative element, inviting us to associate texts, to construct the character's story, and to reinterpret as we read. At the same time, the presence of the reappearing character multiplies the dramatic value of such narrative elements as description, incident, and image by allowing, and at times forcing, us to receive them in the complex context of the ensemble that the single character represents. We become tangibly involved in the work of coproduction. As Michel Butor has stated, our knowledge of the whole is limited within any single part until all pieces of the whole are put together.

> Il ne nous sera donné, concernant tel ou tel, que ce qu'il est indispensable de connaître pour une compréhension superficielle de l'aventure en question; et il nous sera possible d'aller plus loin grâce à la lecture des autres livres dans lesquels ces mêmes personnages apparaissent, de telle sorte que la structure et la portée de tel ou tel roman individuel se transforme selon le nombre d'autres romans que nous avons lus; telle histoire qui nous a semblée linéaire et un peu simplette à notre première lecture lors de notre ignorance du monde balzacien, se révèle plus tard comme le point de rencontre de tout un ensemble de thèmes déjà explorés par ailleurs.[4]

> (We will only be given that which is indispensable about this or that character for a superficial understanding of the adventure in question; and, thanks to the reading of other books in which these same characters appear, it will be possible for us to go further in such a way that the structure and the significance of any individual novel transforms itself according to the number of other

novels that we have read. One story, which at our first reading and in our ignorance of Balzac's world seemed linear and a little silly, reveals itself later as the meeting place of a whole assembly of themes that have already been explored elsewhere.)

The process described by Butor can be illustrated by relating two novels, *Le Père Goriot* and *La Maison Nucingen*. In the latter, we learn that the love affair between Eugène de Rastignac and Delphine de Nucingen, which is portrayed in *Le Père Goriot*, was in fact masterminded, unbeknownst to those involved, by the Baron de Nucingen. That important detail is not even implied in *Le Père Goriot*, and learning it forces us to reconsider the events of that story and to re-evaluate the character of the young Rastignac. On the other hand, of course, if we have not read *Le Père Goriot*, the reading of *La Maison Nucingen* will color our eventual interpretation of it. Finally, the reader who never reads *La Maison Nucingen* will always conceive of Rastignac differently from the reader who knows both. A single detail thus engages us on several levels: it adds to the story that we are compiling of the young Rastignac; it forces us to reinterpret *Le Père Goriot* or influences our future interpretation of it; it links the two works, not only through the character of the Baron de Nucingen who appears in both, nor solely through the character of Rastignac, but also through the evolving and complicated story of the relationship between the two.

So as we read, we expand our understanding, forming the network of relationships composing the whole of *La Comédie humaine*, which always exists in a dynamic state of reconstruction and reproduction. Each text in which one of these characters plays a role can be fully meaningful for a given reader only when all others related to it have also been read. Because of the demand made upon us for an unusually dynamic reading, as we read we sense both the process of creation that mastery of *La Comédie humaine* entails and also the design of the whole. The technique encourages us to expand the boundaries of individual narrations in a unique way, limited only by the confines of our imagination and guided carefully by the system of clues and references contained in the works themselves.

To examine *La Comédie humaine* from the point of view of this unifying technique and the relationship it creates between reader and text is to be made aware of the intricate and meticulous construction upon which Balzac's work rests. The subtle use of what Gerald Prince has called "presupposition," the incorporation of an implicit message into the explicit one,[5] guides us through the network of relationships without taking away from our reading of any given text. Although the reappearing character does not always function on the linguistic level described by Prince, the fundamental technique operates in the same way. The mere presence of a reappearing character, with all the meaning that character may have for us from another novel or story, adds significance to the text being read, incorporating implicitly, and at times almost imperceptibly, the message from a former text. Maurice Bardèche pointed out, for example, in *Balzac romancier* that the presence of the character Gobseck in the home of Mme de Restaud in *Le Père Goriot* permitted Balzac to imply that she needed money.[6] Through this type of subtle manipulation of the reappearing characters, Balzac was able to shape our perception of plots, descriptions, and the characters themselves, in such a way that the manipulation is barely perceptible to us. The use of reappearing characters, then, provided the author with an extraordinarily economical means of representation, because the subordination of the implicit message to the level of narration most prominent in our reading allowed Balzac to suggest new or more subtly nuanced levels of meaning, to reinforce meaning put forth elsewhere, to incorporate an entirely new level of narration within the text being read, or to suppress discourse or explanation, thus accelerating the rhythm of the narration. In Balzac's fiction, then, the reappearing character has proved to be a highly effective tool for directing readers as well as for representation.[7] For us, this literary technique becomes the tool by which we gain a mastery of the total work and the point of departure for our highly creative reading.

La Comédie humaine requires an unusually active reader, and the process by which the total work is read significantly complicates the concepts of "theme" and "horizon" that Wolfgang Iser has proposed as the bases of reading an individual text. According to Iser, a structure of theme and horizon organizes the attitude of the reader and builds up a system of perspectives within our reading of an individual text.

> As perspectives are continually interweaving and interacting, it is not possible for the reader to embrace all perspectives at once, and so the view he is involved with at any one particular moment is what constitutes for him the "theme." This, however, always stands before the "horizon" of the other perspective segments in which he had previously been situated. . . . Now the horizon is not a purely optional one; it is made up of all those segments which had supplied the themes of previous phases of reading.[8]

The structure of theme and horizon is, of course, more complex within La Comédie humaine, in which the reader must consider a wider range of horizons. We attend to the text at hand (that perspective being a theme in Iser's terms), bearing in mind the context of the whole (the horizon of our reading), and eventually place the text with its many components into the multidimensional structure of the whole, where it in turn becomes part of the horizon of our subsequent readings. A single perspective, when it entails the reappearing character, opens onto multiple horizons within not one text but many. Iser believes that the functioning of this dynamic structure is essential for comprehension of the text: "The structure of theme and horizon constitutes the vital link between text and reader, beccause it actively involves the reader in the process of synthesizing an assembly of constantly shifting viewpoints, which not only modify one another but also influence past and future syntheses."[9]

The synthesis of which he spoke, however, is all the more creative in our reading of La Comédie humaine. At all times, we work with at least three levels of narration, each with its own horizons: the text being read; characters and their own stories; and La Comédie humaine as a complete text, a fictional universe. By virtue of this dynamic structure, each appearance of a character becomes both a reflection and an illumination of other appearances. The ultimate meaning of La Comédie humaine as a whole or of any of its parts transcends its individual, determinate elements. The structure further permits a constant enrichment for the reader whose perspectives are broadened and refined at each phase of reading. In Iser's model, the aesthetic object is gradually formed through the accumulation of perspectives and their assembly into a whole (the gradual production of the network of relationships that unifies *La Comédie humaine* into the "fictional mobile" that it is). Slowly, the reader gains a mastery and an overview of the entire work, a vantage point from which to observe the fictional universe.

If we accept the idea that the reading process involved in integrating the reappearing character is based on and yet broadens the structure of theme and horizon, perspective arrangements (Iser defined four of them[10]) take on new meaning. In the first, "counterbalance," a hierarchy of perspectives forms. Balzac skillfully used the second, "oppositional," in which one perspective opposes another, when he placed the story of Horace Bianchon beside that of another character in order to serve as commentary upon the latter. The third, the "echelon" arrangement of references and perspectives, allows none to predominate; instead, each negates, neutralizes, or contradicts another, as occurs with the unfolding of the character and story of Jacques Collin. The last, the "serial," offers a changing perspective from one sentence to the next and requires that we determine both the nature of the perspective and its referential context. This arrangement is the foundation of the presentation that Rastignac receives throughout *La Comédie humaine.*

Perhaps our most significant act in developing a complete picture of any character within the larger context is filling the many gaps that Balzac left to entice us. Iser has called these gaps "indeterminate elements," each one a "switch that activates the reader in using his own ideas in order to fulfill the intention of the text."[11] Through the subjective contribution they encourage us to make, we lend consistency to the character. The positioning of these gaps, of course, is part of the author's overall design, and the material with which we are supplied becomes the guide for our subjective completion of the blank space. According to Iser, indeterminacy, which is present in all literature but striking in Balzac's work, serves many functions within the text and in relation to the reader: it permits readers to organize the referential field for their interpretations; it permits them to grasp or produce a determinate relationship between the segments that surround the indeterminacy; it enables them to engage in a process of "reciprocal modification."[12] Furthermore, the measure of indeterminacy that Balzac integrated into the development of his characters contributes significantly to the illusion of reality surrounding them. In part, we render them lifelike with our subjective contribution to their image: "it is only when the reader is given the chance to participate actively that he will regard the text, whose intention he himself has helped to compose, as real."[13]

The illusion of reality is not, of course, totally the creation of an imaginative reader. That Balzac's characters are lifelike is as much due to their careful and consistent development throughout *La Comédie humaine,* a development that helps to shape our image of them, as it is due to our completion of their stories. There is, in the character of the young Rastignac presented in *Le Père Goriot,* for example, all the potential for the older character we find elsewhere.[14] Combined, consistency of presentation and indeterminacy guide us in our elaboration of his character. The very breadth of the development of these characters, however, assures that their total image will be a blend of material provided by the author and that which we ourselves create. The technique of the reappearing character, as it engages us in the reconstruction of *La Comédie humaine,* draws us gradually into the act of creation, coproduction, by reducing the distance between ourselves and the text. The system of reappearing characters that permits us to unify Balzac's total work is the key to our mastery of *La Comédie humaine.*

Four different reappearing characters will be examined here, each of whom requires a different form of participation from the reader for actualization. Balzac used each differently in establishing an axis of communication between himself and his reader, thereby engaging and guiding us in our reading of these four characters in fundamentally different ways. I shall use as a starting point *Le Père Goriot* because all four appear in it. Although it is not necessarily the cornerstone of *La Comédie humaine*, focusing upon it permits us to see how several texts can relate to, complement, and expand upon a central one.

Horace Bianchon

The identity of Horace Bianchon is fixed within *La Comédie humaine* and changes only slightly over the course of the twenty-nine narrations in which he appears.[15] But that fixed identity is replete with the qualities of goodness, intelligence, humanism, and scientific curiosity, which are, for many readers, the essence of Horace Bianchon. By virtue of Balzac's consistent emphasis upon these qualities, the character takes on a symbolic value within Balzac's work as their embodiment. A few examples will suffice to demonstrate how Balzac made use of Bianchon's fixed identity and its symbolic value to highlight other aspects of his work and to engage his reader in creative response.

Bianchon, although not a central character in *Le Père Goriot*, is fully portrayed there as a bright, inquisitive, witty, and sensitive young medical student. All these traits will be repeatedly reinforced in *La Comédie humaine*. Nearly each time the character appears, it is in some way stressed that he is the humanist doctor, the astute scientist, the clever raconteur, or the faithful friend.[16] In *Le Père Goriot*, Bianchon's identity is perhaps best summed up in the famous passage in which he finds Rastignac in the throes of making a difficult decision.

> "Où as-tu pris cet air grave? lui dit l'étudiant en médecine en lui prenant le bras pour se promener devant le palais.
> — Je suis tourmenté par de mauvaises idées.
> — En quel genre? Ça se guérit, les idées.
> — Comment?
> — En y succombant.
> — Tu ris sans savoir ce dont il s'agit. As-tu lu Rousseau?
> — Oui.

— Te souviens-tu de ce passage où il demande à son lecteur ce qu'il ferait au cas où il pourrait s'enrichir en tuant à la Chine par sa seule volonté un vieux mandarin, sans bouger de Paris.

— Oui.

— Eh bien?

— Bah! J'en suis à mon trente-troisième mandarin.

— Ne plaisante pas. Allons, s'il t'était prouvé que la chose est possible et qu'il te suffit d'un signe de tête, le ferais-tu?

— Est-il bien vieux, le mandarin? Mais, bah! jeune ou vieux, paralytique ou bien portant, ma foi . . . Diantre! Eh bien, non.

— Tu es un brave garçon, Bianchon. (3:164)

("Why are you looking so serious?" asked the medical student, taking his arm. They began to stroll up and down in front of the palace.

"I'm tormented by wicked impulses."

"What sort? You can cure impulses, anyway."

"How?"

"By giving in to them."

"You laugh only because you don't know what I'm talking about. Have you ever read Rousseau?"

"Yes."

"Do you remember that passage where he asks the reader what he would do if he could get rich by killing an old mandarin in China without moving from Paris, just by willing it?"

"Yes."

"Well?"

"Pooh! I've got through thirty-two mandarins already."

"Don't joke about it. Come, if it were proved to you that you could do it—just by a nod of the head, would you?"

"Is he a very old mandarin? . . . Well, anyway, young or old, paralytic or healthy, of course I . . . well, damn it, no, I wouldn't."

"You are a fine, noble boy, Bianchon.")[17]

Portraying the young Bianchon in this novel, Balzac stressed his scientific curiosity and skill in his treatment of the ailing Goriot and his basic humanism when he and Rastignac scrape together enough money to bury the old man. As the character unfolds, each trait to be used elsewhere in *La Comédie humaine* is carefully developed, and it is in this novel that we are given our clearest and longest look at the character.

In some texts in which Bianchon appears, these traits are merely reinforced. In *Illusions perdues*, for example, we read, "Bah! il sera, dit Lousteau, tout de même un grand médecin" (5:477) ("All the same," said Lousteau, "he'll make a great doctor," p. 395). But in *Illusions perdues* we also find a description of Bianchon that is more subtle in its use of the character's identity.

> Parmi ceux qui vivent encore était Horace Bianchon, alors interne à l'Hôtel-Dieu, devenu depuis l'un des flambeaux de l'École de Paris, et trop connu maintenant pour qu'il soit nécessaire de peindre sa personne ou d'expliquer son caractère et la nature de son esprit. (5:315)

> (Among those still alive was Horace Bianchon, then a house-surgeon at the Hôtel-Dieu, who has since become a foremost luminary in the Paris School of Medicine: he is too well-known today for it to be necessary to give a portrait of him or to detail his character and mental qualities.)[18]

We are reminded of the Bianchon of *Le Père Goriot* and receive a glimpse of his progress. But Balzac has enticed us to imagine that progress precisely by denying us his story, by creating a blank space to be filled. The passage stresses in a subtle way two essential traits of the character's identity, his intelligence and his prominence. But more important is the use Balzac made of that identity, having it serve as commentary on the context into which it enters. In *Illusions perdues*, as elsewhere in *La Comédie humaine*, Bianchon lends his prestige and an air of dignity to his surroundings.

In several novels and stories, Balzac stressed Bianchon's reputation as a skillful raconteur. For those of us familiar with that reputation, the introduction of Bianchon as narrator produces the expectation of an entertaining tale. The use of the character in this way, then, allows Balzac to set the tone simply and economically for the narration and to predispose the reader to what is to come. That is certainly the case in *Autre Etude de femme*, as well as in the short story entitled "Etude de femme." Perhaps the most interesting use of Bianchon's identity as skillful raconteur, however, is found in *La Muse du département*. The reader finds not only the evocation of a familiar tale but also a clever use of Bianchon's reputation.

> "Bah! j'ai mieux à vous raconter, dit Bianchon.
> — Voyons," dirent les auditeurs à un signe que fit Lousteau pour dire que Bianchon avait sa petite réputation de conteur.

Dans les histoires dont se composait son fonds de narration, car tous les gens d'esprit ont une certaine quantité d'anecdotes comme Mme de la Baudraye avait sa collection de phrases, l'illustre docteur choisit celle connue sous le nom de *La Grande Bretèche* et devenue si célèbre qu'on en a fait au Gymnase-Dramatique un vaudeville intitulé *Valentine* (voir *Autre étude de femme*). Aussi est-il parfaitement inutile de répéter ici cette aventure, quoiqu'elle fût du fruit nouveau pour les habitants du château d'Anzy. Ce fut d'ailleurs la même perfection dans les gestes, dans les intonations qui valut tant d'éloges au docteur chez Mlle des Touches quand il la raconta pour la première fois. Le dernier tableau du Grand d'Espagne mourant de faim et debout dans l'armoire où l'a muré le mari de Mme de Merret, et le dernier mot de ce mari répondant à une dernière prière de sa femme: "Vous avez juré sur ce crucifix qu'il n'y avait là personne!" produisit tout son effet. Il y eut un moment de silence assez flatteur pour Bianchon. (4:687–88)

("Oh! I can tell you a better story than that." said Bianchon.
"Let us hear," said the audience, at a sign from Lousteau conveying that Bianchon had a reputation as a storyteller.
Among the stock of narratives he had in store, for every clever man has a fund of anecdotes as Madame de la Baudraye had a collection of phrases, the doctor chose the one known as "La Grande Bretèche" and now so famous that it was staged at the *Gymnase-Dramatique* under the title of *Valentine*. So it isn't necessary to repeat it here, though it was new to the inhabitants of the Chateau d'Anzy. And it was told with the same finish of gesture and tone that had won such praise for Bianchon when at Mademoiselle des Touches's supper party he had told it for the first time. The final picture of the Spanish aristocrat, starved to death where he stood in the closet walled up by Madame de Merret's husband, and that husband's last word as he replied to his wife's entreaty, "You swore on that crucifix that there was no one in the closet!" produced their full effect. There was a silent moment highly flattering to Bianchon.)

Everything in this passage is geared to entice us, to attract us to this mysterious tale, and even more so to Bianchon as its narrator. If we are familiar with the story, we are invited to reconstruct and to insert it here, to expand the reading of *La Muse du département* with the recollection of another story, its effect, our role in it, and so on. We are even given more information about this tale and its effect upon the general public to integrate into our conception of it.[19] As he did consistently in passages involving reappearing characters, Balzac accommodated the reader yet to encounter "La Grande

Bretèche." Balzac not only blatantly directed his reader to the source of Bianchon's story, but he also offered a few details to pique the curiosity of the uninformed reader. Even more enticing, however, is the image of Bianchon as narrator, which seems designed to evoke in us the desire to learn more, the very desire that propelled the narration of "La Grande Bretèche" in its complete presentation.

Balzac made another interesting use of Bianchon's fixed identity in *Une Double Famille*, in which he plays a minor role. But it is precisely his personality juxtaposed to that of another character that reveals and highlights the state of that second character. *Une Double Famille* relates the demise of the Comte Roger de Granville, who is embittered by the cruel loss of his mistress, Caroline Crochard. Near the end of the narration, Bianchon encounters the count on the street, and taking him for an old man (so much has his loss changed him), offers him his arm. "Mais, mon cher monsieur, je n'ai encore que cinquante-cinq ans, malheureusement pour moi, répondit le comte de Granville. Un médecin aussi célèbre que vous l'êtes doit savoir qu'à cet âge un homme est dans toute sa force" (2:78) (" 'But my dear monsieur, I am as yet only fifty-five, unfortunately for me,' replied the Comte de Granville. 'A physician as celebrated as you are should know that at that age a man still has all his vigor' "). A long passage follows in which Bianchon reasons with the count who considers his life ended. The conversation between the two characters permitted Balzac to juxtapose two views of life, the count expounding upon his hatred and misery, the doctor presenting his more humanistic philosophy. Trying to arouse once more some feeling in the count, Bianchon recounts to him the story of a young woman who suffers miserably at the hands of her lover. The young woman, however, is Caroline Crochard. The count flies into a rage, the description of which ends with the following:

> Il faudrait qu'un même homme possédât à la fois les crayons de Charlet et ceux de Callot, les pinceaux de Téniers et de Rembrandt, pour donner une idée vraie de cette scène nocturne.
> "Voilà mon compte soldé avec l'Enfer, et j'ai eu du plaisir pour mon argent, dit le comte d'un son de voix profond en montrant

au médecin stupéfait la figure indescriptible du chiffonnier béant. Quant à Caroline Crochard, reprit-il, elle peut mourir dans les horreurs de la faim et de la soif, en entendant les cris déchirants de ses fils mourants, en reconnaissant la bassesse de celui qu'elle aime: je ne donnerais pas un denier pour l'empêcher de souffrir, et je ne veux plus vous voir par cela seul que vous l'avez secourue..."

Le comte laissa Bianchon plus immobile qu'une statue. (2:82–83)

(It would be necessary for a man to possess at once the pencils of Charlet and those of Callot, the brushes of Teniers and of Rembrandt, to give an exact idea of this nocturnal scene.

"There is my account closed with hell, and I have had satisfaction for my money," said the count in the deepest tones of his voice and indicating to the stupefied physician the indescribable countenance of the open-mouthed ragpicker. "As to Caroline Crochard," he went on, "she may die in the horrors of hunger and thirst, with the heartrending cries of her dying sons in her ears, recognizing the baseness of the one whom she loves—I would not give a farthing to prevent her suffering, and I don't want to see you any more if only because you have helped her—"

The count left Bianchon more motionless than a statue.)

In this passage, Horace Bianchon's function goes beyond the simple evocation of an atmosphere. His presence creates a symmetry in the text that no other character could have created as well. The rationality of the doctor contrasts with the irrational behavior of the count. The former's humanism clashes with the latter's hatred. Balzac could have used any character to draw the contrast, but the use of Bianchon is most effective because he symbolizes traits opposite to those made manifest by the count. The presence of Bianchon and all that he represents puts into sharp relief the state of the count, and, therefore, the conclusion of his story. The subtle effect of the juxtaposition of these two characters, of course, is striking only to the reader engaged in the active work of coproduction. The essential meaning of the text is not dependent upon the reader's familiarity with Bianchon. But certainly for those who know him, this passage heightens the effect of the portrayal of the count.

Compared with the activities that other reappearing characters engage us in, our participation vis-à-vis Bianchon is rather simple. We are called upon to recognize the symbolic value that he carries in *La Comédie humaine* and, in that light, to interpret the meaning of his presence in any given text. Bianchon appears repeatedly to create an atmosphere, to comment upon some other element in the narration, or to build expectations in the reader as to the nature of the text. All of this is possible because Bianchon has no story of his own; he is principally an identity manipulated by Balzac to illuminate other characters, other themes, and his powers grow as we become increasingly familiar with his traits.

Madame de Beauséant

Like Horace Bianchon, Mme de Beauséant is a character of fixed identity within *La Comédie humaine.* Balzac used her similarly to Bianchon, but added to her identity a central story that the reader must piece together. The identity with which she is most associated and that Balzac stresses in her numerous appearances is that of grande dame of *Le Père Goriot.* In that novel, one of the two in which she figures prominently, the author presents her to us slowly, emphasizing first her family name, wealth, and social status, and all that her name could do for the young Rastignac.

> *Parent de Mme la vicomtesse de Beauséant par les Marcillac!* ces mots, que la comtesse prononça presque emphatiquement, par suite de l'espèce d'orgueil qu'éprouve une maîtresse de maison à prouver qu'elle n'a chez elle que des gens de distinction, furent d'un effet magique, le comte quitta son air froidement cérémonieux et salua l'étudiant. . . . Ce coup de baguette, dû à la puissante intervention d'un nom, ouvrit trente cases dans le cerveau du Méridional. (3:99)

> *(Related to Madame la Vicomtesse de Beauséant through the Marcillacs!* These words, which the countess uttered in a slightly emphatic way, with the pride that a hostess feels in proving that only people of distinction are allowed in her house, had a magical effect. The count's coldly formal manner vanished, and he returned Eugène's bow. . . . The powerful mediation of a name had, like a magic wand, unlocked thirty pigeonholes in the southerner's brain. (p. 64)

This name, referred to repeatedly in *La Comédie humaine* and always producing the wonderful effect that it does for

Rastignac, becomes one of the symbols in *Le Père Goriot* of the world of Parisian high society. "Elle était d'ailleurs, et par son nom et par sa fortune, l'une des sommités du monde aristocratique" (3:76) ("Moreover she was, both by title and by fortune, one of the leaders of the aristocratic world," p. 38). In *Le Père Goriot*, we come to know Mme de Beauséant along with the main character, Eugène de Rastignac, and only gradually is her wealth and social status paralleled by the personal charm and dignity that round the character out. It is significant that the two facets of the character's identity are developed separately, because Balzac often used them separately in other works. Through the simple evocation of her magical name, we conjure up an image of the highest level of Balzac's fictional society, an image carefully drawn for the reader in *Le Père Goriot*. Elsewhere Mme de Beauséant's charm and grace are called forth, portraying her as aristocratic in nature as well as in name. It is in *Le Père Goriot*, however, that we have one of the most complete portrayals of her identity, developed through the story of her disastrous love affair and her relationship with Rastignac. The former, of course, is the first episode in her personal two-part tale.

The story of her being abandoned by her lover, Ajuda-Pinto, and her subsequent decision to quit Parisian society for isolation in Normandy is well known. The dramatic scene of her farewell, in which her social and personal superiority and the tragedy of her abandonment are stressed, leaves us with a rich portrayal of Mme de Beauséant. All sides of her identity are represented, forming a vivid image of all that she symbolizes in *La Comédie humaine*. Balzac closed the first episode of her story with her departure, but that closing is an invitation to follow Mme de Beauséant in all her majesty to her new home in Normandy. There, in "La Femme abandonnée," we find the second episode of her story. The picture of superiority and triumph that Balzac reinforced so strongly in *Le Père Goriot* contrasts sharply to her next appearance, however.

The full meaning of the second text is only realized when it is seen in tandem with *Le Père Goriot*. The second episode of her story, in many ways a mirror image of the first, is all the more tragic precisely because it recounts her second disastrous love affair. To reinforce the link between the two texts, Balzac opened "La Femme abandonnée" with a summary of *Le Père Goriot* (thereby accommodating his uninformed reader), presenting more data to be integrated into the whole image by offering us an epilogue to the story of the love affair that caused Mme de Beauséant's withdrawal from society. We learn of her isolation in Normandy, as well as the reaction of the society that she has left behind.

> M. de Nueil ignorait que Mme de Beauséant se fût réfugiée en Normandie après un éclat que la plupart des femmes envient et condamnent, surtout lorsque les séductions de la jeunesse et de la beauté justifient presque la faute qui l'a causé. Il existe un prestige inconcevable dans toute espèce de célébrité, à quelque titre qu'elle soit due. Il semble que, pour les femmes comme jadis pour les familles, la gloire d'un crime en efface la honte. De même que telle maison s'enorgueillit de ses têtes tranchées, une jolie, une jeune femme devient plus attrayante par la fatale renommée d'un amour heureux ou d'une affreuse trahison. (2:470)

> (M. de Nueil did not know that Mme de Beauséant had taken refuge in Normandy after a notoriety that most women both envy and condemn, especially when the seductions of youth and beauty almost justify the mistake that caused it. An unbelievable prestige accompanies every kind of fame, no matter what its source. It seems that, for women now, as it used to be for families, the glory of a crime effaces the shame. Just as such and such a noble family was proud of its heads that had fallen on the scaffold, a beautiful young woman becomes more attractive by the dubious renown of a happy love or a scandalous desertion.)

This passage obviously serves as commentary on both texts. In *Le Père Goriot*, her story was told principally through the eyes of Rastignac, but Balzac has added another perspective, that of the Parisian society described in the first text and playing only a minor role in "La Femme abandonnée." Later in the short story, Mme de Beauséant recounts her side of the story, adding yet another point of view. As we combine these perspectives, we cannot help but see the second episode of her story in light of the first.

The presentation of Mme de Beauséant in "La Femme abandonnée" draws directly upon *Le Père Goriot* by calling attention to some small changes in her appearance, which, the narrator would have us believe, are a result of the affair: "la passion qui avait failli lui coûter la vie, et qu'attestaient soit les rides qui, par le moindre mouvement, sillonnaient son front, soit la douloureuse éloquence de ses beaux yeux souvent levés vers le ciel!" (2:476) ("the passion that had nearly cost her her life and that was manifest in either the wrinkles that, in the least little movement, crossed her brow, or the sad eloquence of her beautiful eyes that she frequently raised to heaven!"). With the information the opening provides, we easily complete the gap in her story. Because of the direct link to *Le Père Goriot*, passages occurring early in "La Femme abandonnée" that comment retrospectively on the novel also foreshadow events yet to come in the short story. There is, for example, a long passage in which she explains to Gaston de Nueil why she left Paris (a question that remained unanswered in *Le Père Goriot*), rendering even more tragic her second abandonment. She explains that she cannot continue to receive the young man: to be suspected of a second love affair would make of her "une femme méprisable et vulgaire" ("a contemptible and vulgar woman").

Une vie pure et sans tache donnera donc du relief à mon caractère. Je suis trop fière pour ne pas essayer de demeurer au milieu de la Société comme un être à part, victime des lois par mon mariage, victime des hommes par mon amour. Si je ne restais pas fidèle à ma position, je mériterais tout le blâme qui m'accable, et perdrais ma propre estime. Je n'ai pas eu la haute vertu sociale d'appartenir à un homme que je n'aimais pas. J'ai brisé, malgré les lois, les liens du mariage: c'était un tort, un crime, ce sera tout ce que vous voudrez; mais pour moi cet état équivalait à la mort. J'ai voulu vivre. Si j'eusse été mère, peut-être aurais-je trouvé des forces pour supporter le supplice d'un mariage imposé par les convenances. À dix-huit ans, nous ne savons quère, pauvres jeunes filles, ce que l'on nous fait faire. J'ai violé les lois du monde, le monde m'a punie; nous étions justes l'un et l'autre. J'ai cherché le bonheur. N'est-ce pas une loi de notre nature que d'être heureuses? J'étais jeune, j'étais belle ... J'ai cru rencontrer un être aussi aimant qu'il paraissait passionné. J'ai été bien aimée pendant un moment! ... (2:482–83)

(A pure and blameless life will bring my character into relief. I am too proud not to try to live in society as one apart, a victim of the laws by my marriage, a victim of men by my love. If I were not faithful to my position, I would merit all the blame heaped upon me and lose my self-esteem. I did not have the lofty social virtue to belong to a man I did not love. I have broken the bonds of marriage despite the laws: it was wrong, a crime, everything you wish, but for me the bonds were equal to death. I wanted to live. Had I been a mother, perhaps I would have had the strength to tolerate a marriage of convenience. At eighteen years old, poor girls, we barely know what they would have us do. I have broken the laws of the world; the world has punished me. We have both done rightly. I sought happiness. Isn't it a law of our nature to be happy? I was young, beautiful . . . I believed I had met a being as loving as he seemed passionate. I was indeed loved for a little while.)

Even as this passage adds new depth to the character, it acts as a pivot between her two stories. Mme de Beauséant falls once again in love, is once again abandoned, and for the second time resigns herself to total isolation. The reader is encouraged throughout to view the two affairs side by side, comparing the two portrayals of the woman in love and, especially, contrasting her glorious departure from Paris in *Le Père Goriot* to the total devastation that the second abandonment causes.

Là, il vit à la lueur de deux bougies la marquise maigre et pâle, assise dans un grand fauteuil, le front incliné, les mains pendantes, les yeux arrêtés sur un objet qu'elle paraissait ne point voir. C'était la douleur dans son expression la plus complète. Il y avait dans cette attitude une vague espérance, mais l'on ne savait si Claire de Bourgogne regardait vers la tombe ou dans le passé. (2:501)

(There, by the light of two candles, he saw the marquise, thin and pale, seated in a large armchair, her head bowed, her hands hanging listlessly, her eyes fixed on an object she seemed not to see. Her whole expression spoke of hopeless pain. There was a vague hope in her attitude, but one couldn't tell if Claire de Bourgogne was looking toward the tomb or backward into the past.)

Following the second abandonment, Mme de Beauséant chooses not to flee Normandy as she fled Paris, but to isolate herself even more completely than before. The passage above in which she explains early in "La Femme abandonnée" the reasons for her first flight becomes all the more significant because Balzac expressly denied us any further explanation of her final decision. The narrator announces that the secret behind her behavior will be ours to imagine: "Par une multitude de raisons qu'il faut laisser ensevelies dans le coeur des femmes, et d'ailleurs chacune d'elle devinera celles qui lui sont propres, Claire continua d'y demeurer après le mariage de M. de Nueil" (2:500) ("Claire continued to live there after M. de Nueil's marriage for a number of reasons that are best left buried in the hearts of women. Every woman is free to assign those that most appeal to her").

The distinct suppression of information is, of course, our invitation to fill the gap with our own imaginative response. The final glimpse of the ruined Mme de Beauséant must be integrated into the image we have of her total superiority, using as our guide her explanation of the consequences of a "second mistake." Thus, even at the end of her story, that pivotal passage remains a key to our mastery of it.

In the fictional universe of *La Comédie humaine*, the story of Mme de Beauséant's ultimate downfall is not known to many of the characters (since Gaston de Nueil commits suicide at the end of "La Femme abandonnée"). We enjoy a unique perspective, and our knowledge of the second half of her story adds a certain irony to the acclaim that she enjoys by virtue of the first half. For the attentive reader, the network of relationships at the center of which is this character presents a number of challenges. In *Albert Savarus*, for example, there is a passage that comments directly on, and contradicts, a parallel one in "La Femme abandonnée." While only a very attentive reader will note the parallel, still more information about Mme de Beauséant emerges from the juxtaposition. From *Albert Savarus* we read:

De la villa voisine, où se voit un embarcadère à peu près pareil, s'èlança comme un cygne une yole avec son pavillon à flammes, sa tente à baldaquin cramoisi, sous lequel une charmante femme était mollement assise sur des coussins rouges, coiffée en fleurs naturelles, conduite par un jeune homme vêtu comme un matelot et ramant avec d'autant plus de grâce qu'il était sous les regards de cette femme.

"Ils sont heureux! dit Rodolphe avec un âpre accent. Claire de Bourgogne, la dernière de la seule maison qui ait pu rivaliser la maison de France . . .

— Oh! . . . elle vient d'une branche bâtarde, et encore par les femmes . . .

— Enfin, elle est vicomtesse de Beauséant, et n'a pas . . .

— Hésité! . . . n'est-ce pas? à s'enterrer avec M. Gaston de Nueil, dit la fille des Colonna. Elle n'est que française et je suis italienne, mon cher monsieur." (1:965)

(From the neighboring villa, where the place of embarkation is somewhat similar, a yawl darted forth like a swan, with its flag run up and a crimson awning spread, beneath which a charming woman reclined on crimson cushions, her hair wrapped with natural flowers, while a young man, dressed as a sailor, rowed the boat, with all the more grace because he was doing it under her eyes.

"They are happy!" said Rodolphe, in a bitter tone, "Claire de Bourgogne, the last of the only house that could ever rival the kings of France—"

"Oh! she comes from an illegitimate branch, and even, through its women."

"At any rate, she is the Vicomtesse de Beauséant, and didn't—"

"Hesitate!—right?—to bury herself with Monsieur Gaston de Nueil," said the daughter of the Colonnas. "She is only a French-woman: I am an Italian, my dear friend.")

In "La Femme abandonnée," we find the following passages separated by only a portion of one paragraph:

Une Italienne, une de ces divines créatures dont l'âme est à l'antipode de celle des Parisiennes et que de ce côté des Alpes l'on trouverait profondément immorale, disait en lisant des romans français: "Je ne vois pas pourquoi ces amoureux passent autant de temps à arranger ce qui doit être l'affaire d'une matinée." (2:491)

Mme de Beauséant et M. de Nueil demeurèrent pendant trois années dans la villa située sur le lac de Genève que la vicomtesse avait louée. Ils y restèrent seuls, sans voir personne, sans faire parler d'eux, se promenant en bateau, se levant tard, enfin heureux comme nous rêvons tous de l'être. (2:492)

(An Italian woman, one of these divine creatures whose hearts make them the exact opposite of Parisian women, and who, on this side of the Alps are considered profoundly immoral, made the following comment on some French novels: "I cannot see why these poor lovers spend so much time arranging what ought to be the affair of a morning.")

(For three years Mme de Beauséant and M. de Nueil lived in a villa on Lake Geneva that the Vicomtesse had rented. They stayed alone there, without seeing anyone, causing no one to speak of them, taking boat rides, getting up late. In short, they knew the happiness we all dream of having.)

Obviously, the passage from *Albert Savarus* comments on

and even qualifies the two that parallel it in "La Femme abandonnée." The pride (disdain?) with which the woman says "Elle n'est que française et je suis italienne mon cher monsieur" can be better understood in light of the explanatory passage in "La Femme abandonnée." Taken together, the three passages offer yet another perspective to be integrated into the total image and story of Mme de Beauséant.

Moreover, Balzac used the story of Mme de Beauséant's disastrous love affair with Ajuda-Pinto in another way, as an example of love between unmatched men and women. In *Le Lys dans la vallée*, Félix de Vandenesse asks:

> Quelle singulière et mordante puissance est celle qui perpétuellement jette au fou un ange, à l'homme d'amour sincère et poétique une femme mauvaise, au petit la grande, à ce magot une belle et sublime créature; à la noble Juana le capitaine Diard, de qui vous avez su l'histoire à Bordeaux; à Mme de Beauséant un d'Ajuda, à Mme d'Aiglemont son mari, au marquis d'Espard sa femme? (9:1079)

> (What strange and bitter force is that which always brings together an angel and a fool, a sincere and poetic loving man and an evil woman, the petty man and the great woman, an ape and a sublime and beautiful creature; noble Juana and Captain Diard, whose story you learned in Bordeaux, Mme de Beauséant and d'Ajuda, Mme d'Aiglemont and her husband, the Marquis d'Espard and his wife?)

This passage places the story of Mme de Beauséant into a different context by classifying it within one category of love affairs. To interpret that category, the informed reader will superimpose Mme de Beauséant's story upon the others and upon the narration being read. The uninformed reader, however, will superimpose the story told in *Le Lys dans la vallée* upon the others and will imagine what their nature might be.[20]

The use of Mme de Beauséant, then, requires of us a different sort of creativity from that which Horace Bianchon required, because Balzac added to her fixed identity a story told in two principal parts. Mme de Beauséant becomes an important character because she represents a combination of aristocracy and personal tragedy. Our task is twofold: to grasp the implications of both references and to piece together the developing tragedy. Nonetheless, our participation vis-à-vis this reappearing character is somewhat passive compared to what Jacques Collin and Eugène de Rastignac demand of us.

Jacques Collin

In an article entitled "Balzac et le déchiffrement des signes," Jean-Luis Bourget claimed that "déchiffrement" ("deciphering") is the essential theme, motif, and structure of *La Comédie humaine*, explaining, "Déchiffrer consiste d'abord à savoir compléter un message fragmentaire, à restituer la plénitude du sens, à combler ce qui est ressenti comme un manque, une absence"[21] ("To decipher consists first in knowing how to complete a fragmentary message, to restore the fullness of meaning, to fill what seems to be a lack, an absence"). A character that is certainly one of the most significant metaphors of *déchiffrement* in Balzac's work is Jacques Collin. The participation that he demands of us can best be described as a game in which we pass through several stages of awareness until we finally assume the perspective that was Balzac's own as creator of the complex set of signs and disguises that make up Jacques Collin. A reappearing character significantly different from the others under consideration, he merits special attention because of the communication that he promotes between Balzac and his reader. In the case of Jacques Collin, Balzac has challenged us to a refined game of readership, the rules of which are written into the character's presentation. *Jacques Collin* is a character rarely presented as such in *La Comédie humaine*. Instead, we discover a series of disguises and false identities linked to the name *Collin* by thin clues. The identity and personality of Collin himself are presented to us by the police—who can only suspect that Collin is the character beneath the disguises. Like the police, we must decipher the clues that Balzac carefully laid out and form a composite from the many disguised appearances. Eventually, we are allowed to grasp what the police are unable to see, and we watch the game of *déchiffrement* being played out before us. Once we have decoded Collin's false identities and integrated them into his suspected (that is, real) identity, we view the whole procedure from the opposite side, privy to the code, watching other characters as they try to discover the truth. Thus, what Bourget offered as an essential motif of *La Comédie humaine* is embodied in Jacques Collin and the activity in which he involves us. "Si déchiffrer, c'est littéralement élucider, c'est aussi connaître la face cachée des êtres et des objets, l'envers de la tapisserie"[22] ("If to decipher is literally to elucidate, it is also to know the hidden face of beings and objects, the reverse side of the tapestry").

Jacques Collin is considered one of Balzac's most interesting characters, the criminal-genius. The author could not have established the character as superior to his others, however, had he not guided us first into the game of recognition and then to full recognition and the superior perspective we share with the narrator. The genius of the character emerges as we watch him manipulate his disguises in order to hide his real identity, as we are made to play the game of *déchiffrement*, and as we become aware of the total design of true, false, and suspected identities. As Bourget suggested, the decoding of the character is a reduction of and a parallel to all our activity within *La Comédie humaine*. As in all his fiction, Balzac challenged us to see beyond the surface, to penetrate reality to its essence. Jacques Collin, with his constant enticement to perceive beyond, is a metaphor for the challenge that Balzac extended to us within *La Comédie humaine*, a challenge that he himself accepted, to grasp the essential nature of reality.

The portrayal of Jacques Collin requires a linear or chronological reading that begins with *Le Père Goriot* and continues through *Illusions perdues* and *Splendeurs et misères des courtisanes*. Only in that order can we gather all the clues and false identities, which are brought once again before us in the third novel. With the very first mention of Collin in *Le Père Goriot*, his identity is questionable, and all signs point to a puzzle: "un homme âgé d'environ quarante ans, qui portait une perruque noire, se teignait les favoris, se disait ancien négociant, et s'appelait M. Vautrin" (3:55) ("a man of about forty who wore a black wig, dyed his mustache, described himself as a retired merchant, and gave his name as Monsieur Vautrin," p. 14). The elements of mystery surrounding the character are stressed over and over in *Le Père Goriot*. The most complete description we find of Vautrin strongly shapes our visualization of him, emphasizing a few significant physical features. Its main apparent function, however, is to encourage us to pose questions about him.

Vautrin, l'homme de quarante ans, à favoris peints . . . était un de ces gens dont le peuple dit: "Voilà un fameux gaillard!" Il avait les épaules larges, le buste bien développé, les muscles apparents, des mains épaisses, carrées et fortement marquées aux phalanges par des bouquets de poils touffus et d'un roux ardent. Sa figure, rayée par des rides prématurées, offrait des signes de dureté que démentaient ses manières souples et liantes. Sa voix de basse-taille, en harmonie avec sa grosse gaieté, ne déplaisait point. Il était obligeant et rieur. Si quelque serrure allait mal, il l'avait bientôt démontée, rafistolée, huilée, limée, remontée, en disant: "Ça me connaît." Il connaissait tout d'ailleurs, les vaisseux, la mer, la France, l'étranger, les affaires, les hommes, les événements, les lois, les hôtels et les prisons. Si quelqu'un se plaignait par trop, il lui offrait aussitôt ses services. Il avait prêté plusieurs fois de l'argent à Mme Vauquer et à quelques pensionnaires; mais ses obligés seraient morts plutôt que de ne pas le lui rendre, tant, malgré son air bonhomme, il imprimait de crainte par un certain regard profond et plein de résolution. À la manière dont il lançait un jet de salive, il annonçait un sang-froid imperturbable qui ne devait pas le faire reculer devant un crime pour sortir d'une position équivoque. Comme un juge sévère, son oeil semblait aller au fond de toutes les questions, de toutes les consciences, de tous les sentiments. Ses moeurs consistaient à sortir après le déjeuner, à revenir pour dîner, à décamper pour toute la soirée, et à rentrer vers minuit, à l'aide d'un passe partout que lui avait confié Mme Vauquer. Lui seul jouissait de cette faveur. Mais aussi était-il au mieux avec la veuve, qu'il appelait maman en la saisissant par la taille, flatterie peu comprise! La bonne femme croyait la chose encore facile, tandis que Vautrin seul avait les bras assez longs pour presser cette pesante circonférence. Un trait de son caractère était de payer généreusement quinze francs par mois pour le *gloria* qu'il prenait au dessert. Des gens moins superficiels que ne l'étaient ces jeunes gens emportés par les tourbillons de la vie parisienne, ou ces vieillards indifférents à ce que ne les touchait pas directement, ne se seraient pas arrêtés à l'impression douteuse que leur causait Vautrin. Il savait ou devinait les affaires de ceux qui l'entouraient, tandis que nul ne pouvait pénétrer ni ses pensées ni ses occupations. Quoiqu'il eût jeté son apparente bonhomie, sa constante complaisance et sa gaieté comme une barrière entre les autres et lui, souvent il laissait percer l'épouvantable profondeur de son caractère. Souvent une boutade digne de Juvénal, et par laquelle il semblait se complaire à bafouer les lois, à fouetter la haute société, à la convaincre d'inconséquence avec elle-même, devait faire supposer qu'il gardait rancune à l'état social, et qu'il y avait au fond de sa vie un mystère soigneusement enfoui. (3:60–62)

[Vautrin, the man of forty with the dyed whiskers, . . . was one of those whom the vulgar describe as "a bright spark." He was very muscular, with broad shoulders, a well-developed chest, and thick square hands with prominent tufts of fiery red hair on the fingers. His face was prematurely lined, and the occasional hardness of it was offset by his easy, engaging manners. His deep resonant voice, in keeping with his boisterous gaiety, was in no way displeasing. He was cheerful and obliging. If one of the locks stuck, he would in no time take it to pieces, mend it, oil it, file it, and replace it, with the comment: "I know their little ways."

He knew the ways of a lot of other things too: ships, the sea, France, foreign countries, men, business, the law, current events, mansions, and prisons. If anyone was heard grumbling rather more than usual he was instantly ready to help. He had often lent money to Madame Vauquer and to some of the boarders; but his debtors would sooner have died than not pay him back, for in spite of his friendly manner there was something in his bold searching look that inspired fear. There was an unshakable composure even in the way he spat; he gave you the feeling that to get out of a difficult position he would not stop short of crime. His stern judicial eye seemed to penetrate to the depths of every problem, every moral scruple, every feeling.

His habits were regular: he always went out after breakfast, returned for dinner, disappeared for the whole evening, and let himself in about midnight with a passkey given him by Madame Vauquer. He alone was accorded this privilege. But he was, after all, very much her favorite. He would often call her "Mamma," and throw his arms round her waist. She did not quite realize the exceptional talent involved in this piece of flattery: for simple as the gesture seemed to her, he was, in fact, the only man in the place with arms long enough to go round her waist. It was characteristic of Vautrin that he extravagantly paid fifteen francs a month for the coffee and brandy he took after dinner.

Anyone more observant than his fellow boarders—the young men caught up in the whirl of Parisian life, the older ones indifferent to everything that did not touch them directly—might have wondered a little at the ambiguous impression this man produced.

He knew, or had guessed, the secrets of everyone in the place; his own thoughts and activities no one could fathom. Although his patent good nature, his invariable pleasantness and gaiety, had been erected as a barrier between himself and the others, flashes of the sinister undercurrents in his character were often seen. There were frequent satirical outbursts, some of them worthy of Juvenal, against the absurdities of the law, against high society and its self-contradictions. He evidently bore some deep-rooted grudge against the social order; and somewhere in his life there was a carefully shrouded mystery.) (pp. 19–20)

Our questioning of Vautrin-Collin will be mirrored within the text by a similar curiosity on the part of the other characters. We store clues as we would in a mystery tale and the more we know of the character, the more intriguing does he become. Balzac retained control of our search, however, by offering little information and by simultaneously stressing some important traits: the character's strength, the force of his will, his large hands and shoulders, his audacity, his seeming omniscience, and, most particularly, his piercing gaze. The author stressed these not only through description of the character but also through a portrayal of Vautrin's effect upon others, the narrator's observations, and Rastignac's fear of him.

Within *Le Père Goriot*, Balzac initiated us into one phase of the game surrounding Collin that becomes even more interesting when we are in the position to consider the total design of the character. I refer to the multiplicity of names by which he is called. Each one represents one of his principal disguises or a facet of his identity: Vautrin, "Trompe-la-Mort" ("Cheat-death"), Carlos Herrera, "le masque" ("the mask"), and, finally, Jacques Collin. So mysterious is he, however, that names alone will not do. In *Le Père Goriot*, the narrator also calls him, among many other names, a "sphinx en perruque" (3:133) ("sphinx in a wig"), "le tentateur" (3:163) ("the tempter"), and "ce démon" (3:184) ("this demon"). Vautrin's true identity remains shrouded in mystery, and before it is revealed to us, we see him from all sides and are confronted with several layers of identity (the possible, the probable, the known, and the feared). We must unravel or ferret out the truth about this character and are thus (in *Le Père Goriot*) in the position we will find the police in *Splendeurs et misères des courtisanes*, that is, seeing before us one identity, suspecting another, but unable to penetrate the one before us.

When it seems that Vautrin himself will clear up the mystery by revealing his identity to Rastignac, he does not. Instead, he offers Rastignac a plan for sponsorship that would make the older man patron and behind-the-scenes manager of the young man's life and career, a relationship paralleled later with Lucien de Rubempré in *Illusions perdues* and *Splendeurs et misères*. In this lengthy passage (ten pages), not only did Balzac reinforce the aspects of Vautrin-Collin that we must retain if we are to participate fully in the rest of the game (a massive chest and great strength, omniscience, daring) but he also exposed at length the plan for sponsorship that will be one of the principal clues to our recognition of the character when he reappears in a different disguise.

Another scene in *Le Père Goriot*, the one in which Vautrin is captured, is important because it is our first and last glimpse of the actual Jacques Collin. It is a brief and impressive portrayal of the powerful criminal, and it is the only appearance of him undisguised in all of *La Comédie humaine*.

Accompagnées de cheveux rouge-brique et courts qui leur donnaient un épouvantable caractère de force mêlée de ruse, cette tête et cette face, en harmonie avec le buste, furent intelligemment illuminées comme si les feux de l'enfer les eussent éclairés. Chacun comprit tout Vautrin, son passé, son présent, son avenir, ses doctrines implacables, la religion de son bon plaisir, la royauté que lui donnaient le cynisme de ses pensées, de ses actes, et la force d'une organisation faite à tout. Le sang lui monta au visage, et ses yeux brillèrent comme ceux d'un chat sauvage. Il bondit sur lui-même par un mouvement empreint d'une si féroce énergie, il rugit si bien qu'il arracha des cris de terreur à tous les pensionnaires. A ce geste de lion, et s'appuyant de la clameur générale, les agents tirèrent leurs pistolets. Collin comprit son danger en voyant briller le chien de chaque arme, et donna tout à coup la preuve de la plus haute puissance humaine. Horrible et majestueux spectacle! Sa physionomie présenta un phénomène qui ne peut être comparé qu'à celui de la chaudière pleine de cette vapeur fumeuse qui soulèverait des montagnes, et que dissout en un clin d'oeil une goutte d'eau froide. La goutte d'eau qui froidit sa rage fut une réflexion rapide comme un éclair. Il se mit à sourire et regarda sa perruque. (3:217–18)

(The short red-brick hair gave his face a frightful appearance of cunning strength, matching his huge chest and shoulders. His whole bearing seemed to glow with a fire from hell.

Vautrin was at last revealed complete: his past, his present, his future, his ruthless doctrines, his religion of hedonism, the regality conferred on him by his cynical thoughts and deeds and his devil-may-care strength of character. The blood mounted to his cheeks, and his eyes gleamed like a wildcat's. He sprang back with savage energy and let out a roar that drew shrieks of terror from the boarders. At this tigerish movement, and with the general clamor as their excuse, the officers drew their pistols. Collin recognized his danger the moment he saw the glitter of the steel, and suddenly gave proof of superhuman self-control. A terrifying, majestic sight! His rage suddenly dissolved. It was like the phenomenon produced when a vast caldron of steaming vapor, powerful enough to split a mountain, is dissolved in the twinkling of an eye at the touch of a drop of cold water. The drop of water that cooled Collin's wrath was a lightning thought. He broke into a smile, and looked down at his wig.) (p. 195)

Although we will not again see the character undisguised, we are called upon to recall the image presented in this scene as we identify Jacques Collin through his subsequent disguises. It is therefore fully developed, and the narrator interprets for us what Collin is to represent within Balzac's world.

Le bagne avec ses moeurs et son langage, avec les brusques transitions du plaisant à l'horrible, son épouvantable grandeur, sa familiarité, sa bassesse, fut tout à coup représenté . . . par cet homme, qui ne fut plus un homme, mais le type de toute une nation dégénérée, d'un peuple sauvage et logique, brutal et souple. En un moment Collin devint un poème infernal où se peignirent tous les sentiments humains, moins un seul, celui du repentir. Son regard était celui de l'archange déchu qui veut toujours la guerre. (3:219)

(The prison, with its manners and language, its swift twists from the facetious to the horrible, its appalling grandeur, its familiarity, its depravity, was suddenly demonstrated . . . by this one man. But Collin was no longer a man; he was the epitome of a whole degenerate race, at once savage and calculating, brutal and docile. In a single moment he became a poem from hell, in which all human feelings were painted save one, that of repentance. His expression was that of a fallen archangel bent on eternal war.) (p. 196)

Even with his disguise removed, Jacques Collin remains a mysterious character, and his story clearly does not end with his arrest in *Le Père Goriot*. Because Collin promises to continue his activities, we are left to speculate what his future role will be. Our initiation into Balzac's game guides that speculation, and we know at least that we will find him disguised and will recognize him by using the clues so carefully laid out in *Le Père Goriot*. We next encounter Jacques Collin at the end of *Illusions perdues*. Actually, we meet a character named Carlos Herrera and are given clue after clue that this is Jacques Collin. Although these clues all draw upon the previous disguised identity, nowhere in the text has Balzac explicitly stated that Carlos Herrera is Collin, making the scene most interesting from the point of view of reader participation.[23]

Balzac has designed the presentation of Carlos Herrera in such a way that it stresses the character's physical traits so clearly reinforced in *Le Père Goriot* and even vaguely recalls that novel. As with Vautrin-Collin, an aura of mystery surrounds the Spanish priest, and he has the same effect upon the young Lucien de Rubempré that Vautrin had upon Rastignac. All the clues remain vague, however, until they are put into a context that potentially gives direction to our reading: Carlos Herrera and Lucien ride together in a carriage until they arrive at the property of the Rastignac family where the priest shows considerable interest.

> Le prêtre fit arrêter sa calèche, il voulut, par curiosité, parcourir la petite avenue qui de la route conduisait à la maison et regarda tout avec plus d'intérêt que Lucien n'en attendait d'un prêtre espagnol.
> "Vous connaissez donc les Rastignac? . . . lui demanda Lucien.
> — Je connais tout Paris, dit L'Espagnol en remontant dans sa voiture. (5:695)

> (The priest halted his barouche, wishing out of curiosity to walk along the little avenue from the main road to the manorhouse. He looked at it all with more interest than Lucien would have expected from a Spanish priest.
> "So you know the Rastignacs?" Lucien asked him.

"I know everyone in Paris," said the Spaniard, getting back into the carriage.) (p. 640)

Attentive readers who begin to see the resemblance between Carlos Herrera and Vautrin will not lack clues to guide their elaborations of the parallel between the pairs of men, Carlos Herrera-Lucien and Vautrin-Rastignac. The philosophy that the priest exposes is certainly similar to Vautrin's. The proposition of sponsorship made to Lucien cannot help but remind us of Vautrin's similar proposal to Rastignac. Moreover, the same physical features become material for description:

> Gros et court, de larges mains, un large buste, une force herculéenne, un regard terrible, mais adouci par une mansuétude de commande, un teint de bronze qui ne laissait rien passer du dedans au dehors, inspiraient beaucoup plus la répulsion que l'attachement. (5:705)

> (He was stout and short, with broad hands and broad chest, herculean strength and a glance that terrified, though it could be softened into mildness at will. His bronzed complexion, which allowed nothing to show of what went on inside him, inspired repulsion rather than attachment.) (p. 651)

But the novel ends without clarifying either the identity of this suspicious character or the future of Lucien.

For the reader who does grasp the relationship of Carlos Herrera to Vautrin, the reappearance of Jacques Collin creates an enormous gap between the two texts that it links. Our interpretation of *Illusions perdues* necessarily changes if beneath the disguise of the priest we perceive or suspect the presence of the master criminal. Thus, the questions raised by the reappearance of Collin and his new disguise send us into pure speculation and deciphering. Only when we read a third novel are we given new clues with which to work, however.

The opening of *Splendeurs et misères des courtisanes* is one of the most intriguing within Balzac's work, and certainly it is the high point in our game with Jacques Collin. The juxtaposition of Collin (in yet another disguise) to both Lucien de Rubempré and Eugène de Rastignac forces us to expand our reading to include three texts and three disguises in the moment of our most active *déchiffrement* of Jacques Collin. He appears disguised, a guest at a masked ball at the Opéra. Yet the narrator points out that he is far too evident among the other disguised characters, indeed laughable, because "A de rares exceptions près, à Paris, les hommes ne se masquent point: un homme en domino paraît ridicule" (6:430) ("With a few rare exceptions, men wear no masks in Paris; a man in a domino is thought ridiculous"). Once again, he is linked to a young man, and he is described in terms that are mildly familiar and that encourage us to begin making the series of associations that will connect him to Carlos Herrera, to Vautrin, and ultimately to Jacques Collin. First, the man is described as a "masque assassin, gros et court" (6:430) ("murderous mask, short and stout"), a "masque aux épaules carrées" (6:432) ("square-shouldered mask"), "le masque mystérieux" (6:433) ("the mysterious mask"), and "le gros masque" (6:434) ("the stout mask"). All these phrases emphasize the familiar physical traits of Collin. A more definitive clue, however, is the identity of the young man whom the character is following, Lucien de Rubempré.[24] By extension, then, the "gros masque" may be Carlos Herrera who may be Vautrin who was Jacques Collin. We cannot make the association, however, unless we associated Carlos Herrera with Vautrin when we read *Illusions perdues*.

The most definitive clue we receive is one that recalls for us the relationship between Vautrin and Rastignac. It recreates that twosome and forces us to see as parallel the relationships of Carlos Herrara to Lucien and the masked man to Lucien. When Rastignac makes fun of Lucien he comes face to face with the "masque assassin."

"Jeune coq sorti du poulailler de maman Vauquer, vous à qui le coeur a failli pour saisir les millions du papa Taillefer quand le plus fort de l'ouvrage était fait, sachez, pour votre sûreté personnelle, que si vous ne vous comportez pas avec Lucien comme avec un frère que vous aimeriez, vous êtes dans nos mains sans que nous soyons dans les vôtres. Silence et dévouement, ou j'entre dans votre jeu pour y renverser vos quilles. Lucien de Rubempré est protégé par le plus grand pouvoir d'aujourd'hui, l'Église. Choisissez entre la vie ou la mort. . . .

"Il n'y a que *lui* pour savoir ... et pour oser ... ", se dit-il à lui-même.

Le masque lui serra la main pour l'empêcher de finir sa phrase: "Agissez comme si c'était *lui*", dit-il. (6:434)

("You young cockerel, hatched in Mother Vauquer's coop—you, whose heart failed you when it was time to grab old Taillefer's millions when the hardest part of the business was done—let me tell you, for your personal safety, that if you do not treat Lucien like the brother you love, you are in our power, while we are not in yours. Silence and submission! or I shall join your game and upset the skittles. Lucien de Rubempré is protected by the strongest power of the day—the Church. Choose between life and death. ...."

"No one but *he* could know—or would dare—" he murmured to himself.

The mask clutched his hand tighter to prevent his finishing his sentence.

"Act as if I were *he*," he said.)

The reevocation of the story recounted in *Le Père Goriot*, as well as the reference to the protection of the church, is as explicit as Balzac became in this opening; the passage offers sufficient hints to guide our deciphering of the puzzle. Through our active association of clues and memory of past narrations, then, we can perceive the character as made up of four different identities. Clearly, Balzac relied heavily upon our attentive reading and upon our creativity. Unlike most of the scenes in which reappearing characters appear, the full sense of this opening passage would remain obscure without the active participation of the reader. The identity of the character does, of course, become clear as we read on, and there is no question that *Splendeurs et misères* picks up where *Illusions perdues* has left off, nor that Lucien de Rubempré has accepted the offer of sponsorship that Rastignac refused in *Le Père Goriot*. But the opening passage of *Splendeurs et misères* presents us with both the greatest challenge and the climax of our game of recognition. It forces us to integrate the many disguises with which we have been confronted into a single image of the character. The perspective permitted by integration, moreover, is important to our further participation in the game designed by Balzac.

As the story of *Splendeurs et misères* unfolds, we see the character disguised as Carlos Herrera, but acting out the identity that the police described in *Le Père Goriot*, as Jacques Collin, the master criminal. Because the police suspect that Carlos Herrera is Jacques Collin, alias Vautrin, their investigation keeps before us the two principal disguises as well as the real identity of the character and the three novels in which he has played a role. Nowhere is the presence and the interrelationship of these three texts and the disguises more clearly perceived than in the third section of *Splendeurs et misères* when Jacques Collin is being questioned by the police. Because we have been through the game with which they are now faced (uncovering the real identity of the character and unraveling his disguises), we assume the superior position enjoyed by both the narrator and the author. From that perspective, we are able to see the interplay of real and disguised identities that compose this character and to appreciate the complex narrative design that the preparation of the interrogation scene entailed. The police, however, do not play the game of *déchiffrement* successfully. As in *Le Père Goriot*, the game involves an alternation of names, *Carlos Herrera* and *Jacques Collin* (with an occasional interjection of *Vautrin*). For example, the narrator explains:

> Néanmoins, Jacques Collin ou Carlos Herrera (il est nécessaire de lui donner l'un ou l'autre de ces noms selon les nécessitiés de la situation) connaissait de longue main les façons de la police, de la geôle et de la justice. (6:703)

> (Nevertheless, Jacques Collin, or Carlos Herrera [we must give him one or the other of these names according to the necessities of the situation], was familiar with the methods of police, prison, and justice.)

But, in fact, the use of names is far more subtle than the narrator would have us believe. Their very manipulation forces us to maintain an image of the character in all his poses, an image that integrates the many disguises. When he most cleverly sustains his disguise, making the police doubt their suspicions, the narrator calls him Jacques Collin.

> "Vous êtes soupçonné d'être Jacques Collin, forçat évadé, dont l'audace ne recule devant rien, pas même devant le sacrilège! . . . " dit vivement le juge en plongeant son regard dans les yeux du prévenu.

Jacques Collin ne tressaillit pas, ne rougit pas. (6:747)

("You are suspected of being Jacques Collin, an escaped convict, whose audacity recoils before nothing, not even sacrilege!"—said the judge suddenly, darting his glance into the prisoner's eyes. Jacques Collin did not tremble, his color did not change.)

At other times, the narrator alternates between the two names, thereby altering the perspective of the reader. The following exchange between the police and the criminal demonstrates the way in which different facets of the character can be accentuated by the manipulation of the names.

"Mais si vous êtes Jacques Collin. . . .
Carlos Herrera fut de bronze en écoutant cette phrase. . . .
"Monsieur l'abbé, reprit le juge avec une excessive politesse, si vous êtes don Carlos Herrera. . . .
Jacques Collin devina le piège au seul son de voix du juge quand il prononça *monsieur l'abbé.* (6:750)

("But if you are Jacques Collin. . . .
Carlos Herrera sat like a statue of bronze, listening to this sentence. . . .
"Monsieur l'Abbé," the judge continued, with excessive politeness, "if you are Don Carlos Herrera. . . ."
Jacques Collin discerned a trap by the mere tone in which the judge pronounced the words *Monsieur l'Abbé.*)

Finally, in one segment of the interrogation scene, the identity of Vautrin is also brought into play when the police call upon their informer from *Le Père Goriot*, Mlle Michonneau, to identify the criminal. With much hesitation, she identifies him: "C'est sa carrure, sa taille, mais . . . non . . . si . . . Ah! c'est son regard" (6:756) ("That's his breadth, his height, but . . . no . . . yes . . . Ah! that's his look").

Clearly, then, we must conceive of this character as an assembly of different identities. Unlike other reappearing characters whose stories develop from text to text or whose identities are fixed from one to another, at each appearance Jacques Collin simply offers a new aspect of a single and consistent identity. Ultimately, it is the composite of his masks that becomes the character for us.

Splendeurs et misères ends, as do the other texts in which Jacques Collin appears, upon an invitation to the reader to imagine the continuation of the character's story. To our surprise, he confesses his identity to the police and offers them his services. As the novel ends, he is given a new identity, and it is the new task of the reader to integrate the image of Jacques Collin-*agent de police* into the image that made Collin the symbol of the criminal world. As is common in Balzac's work, there is an epilogue to Collin's story, a single guideline to our final conception of his character. In *La Cousine Bette*, a brief passage involving a character who has been consistently associated with Jacques Collin, his aunt Jacqueline Collin, tells us a little of Collin's career with the police.

Using an alias we encountered in *Splendeurs et misères*, she proposes to members of a family eager to rid themselves of their father's mistress that she and her nephew simply have the woman removed from the scene. The nephew is revealed to be the head of criminal investigation, Jacques Collin, and in this affair we learn, "L'on a donné carte blanche à mon neveu; mais mon neveu ne sera là-dedans que pour le conseil, il ne doit pas se compromettre . . . " (7:386) ("They have given my nephew carte blanche; but he will only advise. He musn't compromise himself . . . "). The reference both creates a gap in Jacques Collin's story that must be completed by the reader and guides us toward that completion. The whole complicated identity that we have assembled for this character may now be brought to bear. Although there are few limitations imposed upon the way we imagine him, Balzac did offer a guide: "Voici quarante ans, monsieur, que nous remplaçons le Destin, répondit-elle avec un orgeuil formidable, et que nous faisons tout ce que nous voulons dans Paris" (7:387) (" 'For forty years now, monsieur, we have been replacing Destiny,' she said with unbelievable pride, 'and doing what we want in Paris' ").

Thus, Jacques Collin requires of the reader some of the same activities as did Horace Bianchon and Mme de Beauséant. Unlike those two, the very identity of the character is what must be assembled, while its symbolic value was clearly established by Balzac early on. The game of recognition that the presentation of Collin-Vautrin-Herrera requires of us, the perspective that it permits us, and the author's careful design and manipulation of the character's multilayered personality make of Jacques Collin one of the most fascinating reappearing characters in *La Comédie humaine.*

Eugène de Rastignac

The presentation of Eugène de Rastignac is quite different from the others, based principally upon the technique of the blank space, the gap, Iser's "indeterminate element." Certainly, of the four characters I examine, and, perhaps of all the reappearing characters, it is this type that fosters the most creative and the most active response from us, because its development requires not only the activities necessary to comprehend Mme de Beauséant and Horace Bianchon but also a far more challenging activity to allow a special mastery of *La Comédie humaine.* In the design of Eugène de Rastignac, Balzac relied more heavily upon the use of implicit messages in order to direct our heightened creativity.

With each appearance of Rastignac, we find him at a different age, social position, or status. Rather than having fixed identity within *La Comédie humaine*, Rastignac has a story, a virtual lifetime of changes, successes, and failures. Although it is surprising how little information Balzac actually supplies us about Rastignac throughout the twenty-three works in which he appears,[25] he is one of the most well known in Balzac's work. In Rastignac, Balzac has created, in essence, the outline of a character whom we complete through our reading. I intend to demonstrate through an analysis of Rastignac how we can participate in the coproduction of him, contribute to the illusion of reality that surrounds him, and thereby gain mastery of *La Comédie humaine.*

Because of the design and presentation of this character, our reading need not follow any specific direction, linear or other. We can begin anywhere in his story and participate in the same ways. As we encounter Rastignac repeatedly, finding him each time at a new place in his story, we begin to complete the huge gaps existing between his appearances. Indeed, that is our principal activity vis-à-vis Rastignac. As we read, we gradually give to the skeletal frame of character and story a fuller shape, incorporating new references where we perceive they belong in a chronology lightly imposed by the author. The activity surrounding the coproduction of this character transcends the reading of any individual narration because its essence is not contained in a single text. In fact, there are references to Rastignac that are far more significant to this other level of narration, his story, than to the text being read. Thus, the completion of Rastignac's story is an activity supplemental to the reading of any single work. Although it does not always strengthen our grasp of the narration being read, it enhances the act of reading—by permitting us to participate simultaneously on two levels, the single narration and the broader structure of *La Comédie humaine.* It is within the broader context, I believe, that the gradual completion of Rastignac's story facilitates a greater mastery of Balzac's work than does that of other reappearing characters. First, it is not limited to just a few narrations but well distributed. Second, it requires that we supply a significantly greater amount of material to the total image of the character.

Although there are three works in which Rastignac plays a major role, in most we see only short glimpses of him or hear reference made to him in passing. More often than not, these references encourage us to pose questions about the character's development. Occasionally, they offer us answers. But with each bit of information, we readjust our image of the character to integrate new material. Even though we may not read Rastignac's story linearly, we must keep before us a linear organization because it is the story of a career that we are constructing. Balzac's choice of details to be revealed and the overall design he gave the character are two of the means by which our reading is guided. The most significant element shaping our conception of the character, however, is the consistency with which the author portrayed him. Although there are some inconsistencies to be found in the character's development, his basic personality remains constant and consistent with the one novel in which that identity is outlined. That text, of course, is *Le Père Goriot,* and it is once again a starting point for an examination of the reappearing character.

In *Le Père Goriot*, Balzac presented Rastignac as a young man making his entry into society and, therefore, at a point of importance in making decisions about his future. Because the decision-making process spans the entire work, Balzac could easily portray all sides of the character, his ambition, his vivid imagination, his social inexperience, his relations with his family and friends, and his naiveté. By fully portraying him as a young man, Balzac laid the groundwork for our conception of him at later stages of development, and, indeed, we find in the Rastignac of *Le Père Goriot* the potential for the Rastignac we find elsewhere. In *Le Père Goriot*, our conception of the character is shaped in such a way that later references to him will recall the image of the young man. The shaping process is carried out principally through a considerable interpretation on the part of the narrator of Rastignac's development and gradual passage from innocence to understanding. At the close of *Le Père Goriot*, Rastignac makes his decision between the hard work of the student's life and the pleasures of Parisian high society and, we may assume, throws himself into the battle of the latter. The groundwork alone for that battle has been laid, and the reader will, from here on out, find only the briefest references to its high points. Thus, *Le Père Goriot* opens onto an enormous area of indeterminacy in pointing us toward Rastignac's future, the story of which is scattered throughout *La Comédie humaine*.

Le Père Goriot provides a psychological composite that can serve as backdrop to each new appearance of the character. The meaning of no one appearance depends on our having read *Goriot*, however, and, in fact, Balzac found numerous ways to fill in the uninformed reader on what happened to the character there. Each phase of development follows and comments upon the challenge that Rastignac launches toward society at the end of *Le Père Goriot*. In *La Peau de chagrin*, for example, we find him just slightly older but considerably less ambitious. He describes himself to Raphaël de Valentin: "Je m'ennuie, je suis désappointé. . . . Au diable! En menant une vie enragée, peut-être trouverons-nous le bonheur par hasard!" (10:192) ("I'm bored and disappointed. . . . Oh damn! maybe in leading a wild life we'll find happiness by chance").

The philosophy of life that Rastignac espouses in this passage is that of the bored and disillusioned cynic, nostalgic for a better time. We are left to imagine just how the character has passed from the ambition and eagerness of *Le Père Goriot* to this. His general attitude comes into focus not only in contrast to that of the novel's intense and idealistic protagonist but also in contrast to his own former ambition and determination.

Balzac used a different technique in *La Maison Nucingen* to advance our construction of Rastignac's story. Other characters, themselves curious about Rastignac's career, piece together bits of information in an effort to impose some order. The author presented them as models of coproducers or as textual images of his readers. Like us, the story's characters must arrange what they know of Rastignac chronologically. As they go about the task, of course, passages like the following provide for us a chronology upon which to build our version of the character's story.

> — Mais comment a-t-il fait sa fortune, demanda Couture. Il était en 1819, avec l'illustre Bianchon, dans une misérable pension du quartier latin; sa famille mangeait des hannetons rôtis et buvait le vin du cru, pour pouvoir lui envoyer cent francs par mois; le domaine de son père ne valait pas mille écus; il avait deux sœurs et un frère sur les bras, et maintenant . . .
>
> — Maintenant, il a quarante mille livres de rentes, reprit Finot; chacune de ses sœurs a été richement dotée, noblement mariée, et il a laissé l'usufruit du domaine à sa mère . . .
>
> — En 1827, dit Blondet, je l'ai encore vu sans le sou.
>
> — Oh! en 1827, dit Bixiou.
>
> — Eh bien, reprit Finot, aujourd'hui nous le voyons en passe de devenir ministre, pair de France et tout ce qu'il voudra être! (6:332)

> ("But how did he make his fortune?" asked Couture. "In 1819 he was in a miserable boarding house in the latin quarter with the illustrious Bianchon. His family ate roasted maybugs and drank local wine in order to send him one hundred francs a month. His father's property wasn't even worth one thousand crowns. He had two sisters and a brother to take care of, and now . . . "
>
> "Now, he has forty thousand francs a year," added Finot. "Both of his sisters have been given a sizeable dowry and have married well, and he has left the life interest of the property to his mother."
>
> "In 1827," said Blondet, "I saw him broke again."

"Oh sure, in 1827," said Bixiou.

"Anyway," added Finot, "today we find him about to become a minister, a *pair de France*, and anything else he would like to be!")

Not only does this passage provide new data and create new gaps, but it also forces us to extend Rastignac's story in several directions at once, as it blends elements of his career with those of his personal life. Even as it connects *la Maison Nucingen* to other works involving Rastignac, including *Le Père Goriot* or *La Peau de chagrin*, it transcends such works by commenting upon and guiding the formation of material that we create for the character. A passage like this one shapes the image that we are in the process of creating even as it forces us to readjust that which we have already formulated of that image. It is extraordinarily economical from the author's point of view as it resurrects and renews former, and here contradictory, appearances of the character, and reminds us of the indeterminacy that engages us in the production of this story. In this way, Balzac can call into play our subjective response and maintain a measure of control over it.

Because Rastignac engages us as subjectively as he does, he takes on a greater familiarity than do other reappearing characters. We get an extremely close look at the character in *Le Père Goriot;* we have also elaborated what we found there in a very personal way. In at least one text, Balzac relied upon that familiarity for interest and effect. In "Etude de femme," in which Rastignac plays a major role, it is partly our familiarity with the character that makes the story humorous and appealing. If we are aware of Rastignac's ambition as a young man, his awkward introduction into Parisian society, and his subsequent successes, this little story of an early social blunder is all the more pleasing for the commentary that it offers on his evolution. No effort is made within the story, however, to explain who this character is or whom he has become in the world of *La Comédie humaine*. The narrator is simply telling a humorous tale for its own sake. A reader who has read other references to Rastignac in Balzac's work has no trouble placing "Etude de femme" chronologically in his story. This is the young Rastignac, who has taken on Parisian society but is still ill prepared to do battle. The narrator

(Horace Bianchon) offers his analysis of Rastignac's naiveté (when the latter awkwardly has admitted to Mme de Listomère his liaison with Delphine de Nucingen).

> Voilà les fautes que l'on commet à vingt-cinq ans. Cette confidence causa une commotion violente à Mme de Listomère; mais Eugène ne savait pas encore analyser un visage de femme en le regardant à la hâte ou de côté. Les lèvres seules de la marquise avaient pâli. Mme de Listomère sonna pour demander du bois, et contraignit ainsi Rastignac à se lever pour sortir. (2:179)

> (These are the mistakes that one makes at twenty-five. This confidence produced a violent emotion in Madame de Listomère. But Eugène did not yet know how to analyse a woman's face by looking at it fleetingly or by giving a side glance. Only the marquise's lips had turned pale. Madame de Listomère rang to ask for wood, and so Rastignac was forced to get up to go.)[26]

Of all of the references to Rastignac in Balzac's work none are so playful in their teasing of the reader as those surrounding the rumors of his marriage. Like the characters who appear in these passages, we become part of a group curious about the event. *Une Fille d'Eve* offers one such reference, from a character who is jealous of everything about Rastignac:

> Rastignac, dont le frère cadet venait d'être nommé évêque à vingt-sept ans, dont Martial de La Roche-Hugon, le beau-frère, était ministre, qui lui-même était sous-secrétaire d'Etat et allait, suivant une rumeur, épouser la fille unique du baron de Nucingen. (2:311–12)

> (Rastignac, whose younger brother had just been named a bishop at twenty-seven, whose brother-in-law, Martial de La Roche-Hugon, was a minister, who was himself under-secretary of state, and who was about to marry [or so they said] the only daughter of the Baron de Nucingen.)

The passage obviously offers more information than just that concerning the marriage, but that is its most enticing piece of news, because many readers would know of his liaisons with the Nucingen family. The rumor resurfaces later in the novel, however, and Balzac is more playful still. The Comtesse de Vandenesse speaks to Madame de Nucingen:

> — Vous donnerez sans doute [cette chambre] à mademoiselle votre fille. On parle de son mariage avec M. de Rastignac."

Le caissier parut au moment où Mme de Nucingen allait répondre,
elle prit les billets et remit les quatre lettres de change.
"Cela se balancera, dit la baronne au caissier. (2:368)

("Certainly, you'll give [this room] to your daughter. Everyone is
talking about her marriage to M. de Rastignac."
The cashier appeared just as Mme de Nucingen was about to
reply. She took the notes and returned the four bills of exchange.
"That will balance," said the baroness to the cashier.)

Despite this near miss, the rumor is nowhere confirmed in
Une Fille d'Eve. In order to satisfy our curiosity, we must read
Le Député d'Arcis in which we find Rastignac and his wife.
Little explanation is given. We read only brief references like,
"Madame de Nucingen avait dîné chez la marquise avec sa
fille, mariée depuis un an au comte de Rastignac" (8:804)
("Madame de Nucingen had had dinner at the home of the
Marquise. She was accompanied by her daughter, married
now for a year to the Count de Rastignac"). We learn not only
that Rastignac has been married but also that he has been
made a count. Both messages, however, are subordinated to
the more important details of the novel. The manipulation of
the rumor of marriage and its subordination to other elements of works that contain it make it an excellent example
of the way we must immerse ourselves in Balzac's fictional
world in order to grasp and to develop a character like Rastignac.
More clearly with this type of character than with others, we
must remain alert to the broad context into which reappearing characters and the works in which they appear both fit.
The design of Rastignac in particular encourages us to read
with special creativity and permits us to dominate in a particularly creative way. Likewise, it offers Balzac a unique
vehicle with which to shape the reception of his work.

An examination of Horace Bianchon, Mme de Beauséant,
Jacques Collin, and Eugène de Rastignac in no way exhausts the
number of narrative strategies behind the use of the reappearing character. It does permit us, however, to examine some
fundamental techniques by which Balzac incorporated and
accommodated within his fiction his readers' subjective re-

sponse and thereby continues to exert a measure of control over the reception of both individual narrations and *La Comédie humaine* as a whole. Furthermore, it permits us to appreciate the complicated design that Balzac used to provide us with the material needed for the unification of his work. Far more than any other element, the reappearing character is the key to our mastery of *La Comédie humaine,* forming a potential network of relationships between and among texts, a network that we activate through our reading and through the many related activities dictated to us by the author.

VI

CONCLUSION

L'oeuvre de Balzac est incomparablement plus
révolutionnaire qu'il n'apparaît à une lecture
superficielle et fragmentaire; parmi les nou-
veautés qu'elle apporte, certaines ont été ex-
ploitées systématiquement au cours du XIXè siècle,
d'autres n'ont trouvé d'échos que dans les
oeuvres les plus originales du XXè, et cette
fécondité est bien loin d'être encore épuisée.

(Balzac's work is incomparably more revolutionary
than it appears at a superficial and fragmentary
reading. Certain of the novelties that
it introduces were systematically exploited
during the nineteenth century, others were
imitated only in the most original works of
the twentieth century, and this fertility is
indeed far from being exhausted.)

Butor, "Balzac et la réalité"

The assumptions upon which I have based this study, as
well as its results, argue against those critics who acknowledge no meaning other than that which the active reader
produces. Equally, I do not presume to know with certitude
what is an author's intended meaning. Only a model that
places the text squarely between its author and its readers can
permit us to see the communication effected through literature. In a given work, of course, are concentrated the means
by which authors can guide readers in their reception and
interpretation of the narration. Nonetheless, the response of
each reader will ultimately be a subjective one. The author

cannot impose on us a specific reading but can shape our individual responses. Thus, the devices by which that manipulation is effected must be woven tightly into the fabric of narration.

I hope to have demonstrated the degree to which Balzac attended to the reception of his texts. His interest in transmitting the literary text is manifest in his experimentation with the means of representation at his disposal, and his accommodation of our response within narrations helps to explain, I believe, our continued fascination with *La Comédie humaine*, the strong sense of reality that we experience as we read, and the familiarity that his fictional world has for us.

Of course, other aspects of Balzac's work could be studied in this light, or those considered here could be examined in greater depth. I can only hope that the image of Balzac as innovative artist who experimented with the balance between authorial control and freedom for the reader will spark further study.

I believe that this type of approach has other advantages. To focus on the text as the place where the activities of author and reader converge to coproduce the meaning of the text is to bring an important aspect of contemporary theory to bear upon some traditional questions of literary criticism. This concentration elucidates fundamental aesthetic features peculiar to the literary work of art. It is a questioning of the basic aesthetic nature of literature in its fullest sense, that is, in relation to both author and reader.

I hope as well that the questions that I have posed in relation to *La Comédie humaine* will likewise be put to texts of other writers. Such examination would not only yield new insight on the creative process in literature in general and in the work of specific authors in particular, but it would also permit a new perspective on the dynamics within some of the great texts of our tradition. Furthermore, a historical analysis on how the games of authorship and readership have changed over time might offer interesting and important information for future study.

Finally, I hope that this study has at least provided a beginning, revealed new complexities in *La Comédie humaine*, and illuminated in a different way the rich potential for the reader's own creativity that these texts allow. It has underscored for me once again the daring with which Balzac created his massive literary world.

NOTES

Notes to Chapter I
Introduction

1. Honoré de Balzac, "Avant-Propos," *La Comédie humaine*, ed. Pierre Georges Castex, Edition de la Pléïade, 1:7–20. All references to Balzac's work in this study are to the new Pléïade edition of *La Comédie humaine* unless otherwise noted. Quotations from it will be followed by an indication of both volume and page numbers.

2. Honoré de Balzac, "Lettres sur la littérature," in *Oeuvres complètes de Honoré de Balzac*, 40:278.

3. For an interesting discussion of this concept, see Peter Brooks, *The Melodramatic Imagination, Balzac, Henry James, Melodrama, and the Mode of Excess*, pp. 110–52.

4. Balzac, "Lettres sur la littérature," 40:289.

5. See Christopher Prendergast, "Balzac and the Reading Public," in *Balzac, Fiction and Melodrama*, pp. 17–38.

6. Ibid., p. 20.

7. Balzac, "Lettres sur la littérature," 40:278.

8. It would be naive to believe that Balzac was totally ignorant of his own audience. As Prendergast pointed out, however, the reading public grew rapidly during the years of Balzac's production. Equally, the popularity of serialization imposed new and different demands upon an author interested in appealing to the taste of the day. Tastes were changing rapidly, in part influenced by the growing industry of literature, which paid little heed to artistic merit.

9. Balzac, "Lettres sur la littérature," 40:287.

10. "Avertissement quasi-littéraire," *Le Cousin Pons*, cited by Prendergast, p. 28.

11. For a complete discussion of Balzac as critic and innovative artist, see Geneviève Delattre, *Les Opinions littéraires de Balzac*.

12. Martin Kanes, *Balzac's Comedy of Words*, p. 219.

13. I. A. Richards, *Practical Criticism*.

14. David Bleich, "The Subjective Paradigm in Science, Psychology and Criticism," *New Literary History*.

15. I am not saying that all readings of a given text are correct. There can and frequently do exist blatant misreadings upon which may rest a very false interpretation. I am speaking here of the interpretation of a competent reader who knows fully the language of the text in all its connotative depth, who brings to the text full communicative skills, and who has a certain degree of literary sophistication and experience.

16. For a clear description of the range of assumptions and practices of these theorists in America, see Steven Mailloux, "Learning to Read: Interpretation and Reader-Response Criticism," *Studies in Literary Imagination* 12 (1979): 93–108.

17. In 1929, Richards was being avant-garde in confronting so directly the question of psychic motivation and subjectivity in critical interpretation. A footnote (on p. 7) reveals to us how these issues were viewed. Comparing the difficulty of dealing with the complex diversity of response to the difficulty of following "the ravings of mania or the dream maunderings of a neurotic," Richards excused himself for the implication and then stated in a footnote, "A few touches of the clinical manner will, however, be not out of place in these pages, if only to counteract the indecent tendencies of the scene. For here are our friends and neighbours—nay our very brothers and sisters— caught at a moment of abandon giving themselves and their literary reputations away with an unexampled freedom. It is indeed a sobering spectacle, but like some sights of the hospital ward very serviceable to restore proportions and recall to us what humanity, behind all its lendings and pretenses, is like."

18. W. K. Wimsatt, Jr., and Monroe C. Beardsley, "The Affective Fallacy," in *The Verbal Icon,* pp. 21–39.

19. Simon Lesser, *Fiction and the Unconscious.*

20. Ibid., p. 21.

21. Norman N. Holland, *The Dynamics of Literary Response.*

22. Norman N. Holland, *5 Readers Reading.*

23. See David Bleich, "The Determination of Literary Value"; "The Subjective Character of Critical Interpretation"; *Readings and Feelings: An Introduction to Subjective Criticism;* "The Subjective Paradigm in Science, Psychology and Criticism"; and *Subjective Criticism.*

24. Bleich, "The Subjective Character," p. 745.

25. Walter J. Ong, "The Writer's Audience is Always a Fiction."

26. Wolfgang Iser, *The Implied Reader: Patterns of Communication in Prose Fiction from Bunyan to Beckett.*

27. Wolfgang Iser, *The Act of Reading: A Theory of Aesthetic Response.*

28. Iser, *The Implied Reader,* p. 279.

29. Wolfgang Iser, "La Fiction en effet," p. 279.

30. Iser, *The Act of Reading,* p. 151.

31. Obviously, when we study a text we have more to draw upon than the simple word. We have the author's other writings, our other readings, dictionaries, biographies, and histories. I refer here to that inevitable first reading, to a reading when our major involvement is with the text itself. At that time, our emotional involvement may be at its highest.

32. Iser, *The Act of Reading,* p. 112.

33. Sigmund Freud, *Beyond the Pleasure Principle,* in *The Standard Edition of the Complete Psychological Works of Sigmund Freud,* trans. and ed. James Strachey, 18:7–64.

34. Sigmund Freud, "Creative Writers and Day-Dreaming," 9:143–53.

35. Freud, *Beyond the Pleasure Principle,* 18:62.

36. Wayne C. Booth, *The Rhetoric of Fiction,* pp. 138–39.

37. Gérard Genette, *Figures III,* pp. 265–67. In English, the term *"narrataire"* translates as the rather awkward *"narratee."* Cf. Gerald Prince, "Notes Towards a Categorization of Fictional 'Narratees'," *Genre* IV (1971): 100–5.

38. Ong, "The Writer's Audience," p. 12.

39. Holland, *5 Readers Reading,* p. xii.

40. Iser, *The Implied Reader,* p. 287. Iser used as a primary example of this aesthetic experience James Joyce's *Ulysses,* which encourages a pattern of response but immediately destroys it with each new chapter.

Notes to Chapter II
The Creation of the Referent

1. Michel LeGuern, *Sémantique de la métaphore et de la métonymie*, p. 11. The definition is from Dumarsais, *Traité des tropes*, II:10.

2. LeGuern, p. 16.

3. These three terms are taken from Umberto Eco, *The Role of the Reader*, pp. 82–83. For Eco, the artistic message must contain certain degrees of ambiguity, tension, and difficulty vis-à-vis the recipient if it is to be successful and rewarding.

4. In *The Role of the Reader*, Eco maintained that every metaphor has at its source a series of metonymic links and that it is the task of the reader to uncover them. While I am not convinced of the accuracy of this generalization, I find it most helpful to conceive of the reader's activity as one of detailed and multilayered linkage.

5. Lucienne Frappier-Mazur, *L'Expression métaphorique dans "La Comédie humaine."*

6. See "Notes et variantes," *César Birotteau*, 6:1202–3.

7. Honoré de Balzac, "Notes philosophiques," *Oeuvres complètes*, 25:555, cited and discussed by Martin Kanes in *Balzac's Comedy of Words*, p. 38.

8. See "Notes et variantes," *César Birotteau*, 6:1202–3.

9. *Lettres à Mme Hanska*, 1:554, cited by René Guise, 6:1203.

10. Kanes, *Balzac's Comedy of Words*, p. 115.

11. Paul Ricoeur, *La Métaphore vive*, p. 102. This is an invaluable study for anyone interested in the theory of metaphor.

12. Ibid., p. 115. This concept is from Max Black, *Models and Metaphors* (Ithaca: Cornell University Press, 1962), p. 43.

13. Kanes, *Balzac's Comedy of Words*, p. 131.

14. Without a doubt, there are references in this passage to a reality outside the text, to the florentine baptistry doors, for example, or to the violinist Habeneck, a contemporary of Balzac's. While a knowledge of the cultural references does enhance our understanding of the passage, the development of the metaphor is not in any way dependent on them. Despite these cultural references, the unity of the image remains intratextual. The English version of this passage and of the one on page 35 are from *Rise and Fall of César Birotteau*, translated by Katharine Prescott Wormeley (Boston: Hardy, Pratt and Co., 1886).

15. We read finally of César's death in this sentence: "Un vaisseau s'était déjà rompu dans sa poitrine, et, par surcroît, l'anévrisme étranglait sa dernière respiration" (6:312) ("A vessel had already burst in his chest, and, in addition, the aneurism choked off his last breath").

16. Kanes, *Balzac's Comedy of Words*, p. 199.

17. Ricoeur, *La Métaphore vive*, p. 301.

Notes to Chapter III
A Map to Guide Us

1. David Bellos, "Balzac, Stendhal et le public à l'epoque du réalisme," *Stendhal-Balzac, réalisme et cinéma: Actes du XIe Congrès international stendhalien, Auxerre, 1976*, ed. Victor del Litto, p. 29. Bellos based his claim

on the fact that during these years a high number of Balzac's works were published: "plus de cinquante volumes enregistrés à la *Bibliographie de la France* par la seule année 1857" ("more than fifty volumes registered in the *Bibliographie de la France* for 1857 alone").

2. There has been a great deal of work done on descriptions in *La Comédie humaine:* Patrick Imbert, *Sémiotique et description balzacienne;* Jean-Pierre Richard, *Etudes sur le romantisme,* pp. 7–139; Bernard Vannier, *L'Inscription du corps: Pour une sémiotique du portrait balzacien;* Tahsin Yücel, *Figures et messages dans "La Comédie humaine."*

3. For an interesting discussion of the importance and functioning of opening signals, see Victor Brombert, "Opening Signals in Narrative."

4. Philippe Hamon, "Qu'est-ce que c'est qu'une description?" p. 482.

5. Ibid., pp. 465–68.

6. Roland Barthes, "L'Effet du réel," p. 85.

7. Hamon, "Qu'est-ce que c'est," p. 474.

8. Ibid., p. 477.

9. Imbert, *Sémiotique et description balzacienne,* pp. 15–16.

10. René Wellek and Austin Warren have written, "Setting is environment; and environments, especially domestic interiors, may be viewed as metonymic, or metaphoric, expressions of character" *(Theory of Literature,* p. 221). From the perspective of the reader, we can expand this concept to add that the description of setting is a metonymic or metaphoric demonstration of the activity of the reader.

11. Gérard Genette, "Frontières du récit," p. 61.

12. Honoré de Balzac, "Lettres sur la littérature," p. 283. The translation of this passage is from Katharine Prescott Wormeley, *Honoré de Balzac, Personal Opinions* (New York: George D. Sproul, 1905), p. 116.

13. Robert Alter, *Partial Magic: The Novel as Self-Conscious Genre,* p. 87.

14. Ibid., p. 93.

15. Pierre Laubriet, *L'Intelligence de l'art chez Balzac,* pp. 64–65.

16. For a discussion of Balzac's ideal of artistic genius (as he perceived it in Molière), see Geneviève Delattre, *Les Opinions littéraires de Balzac,* pp. 80–82.

17. Madeleine Fargeaud saw this statement as a response by Balzac to the mockery of a number of journalists, to a criticism of *Eugénie Grandet* that complained of "quelques longueurs, quelques descriptions un peu trop minutieuses" ("a few passages too long, a few descriptions a little too minute") (*Revue de Paris,* janvier 1834). She linked the defense found in *La Recherche de l'absolu* to a similar one in "La Préface d'*Une Fille d'Eve,*" 2:266–67. Cf. "Notes et variantes," *La Recherche de l'absolu,* 10:1578–79.

18. Fargeaud related this analogy to the science of Cuvier, the founder of comparative anatomy and a scientist for whom Balzac had great admiration. "On connaît le culte de Balzac pour celui qu'il appelle 'l'enchanteur' dans *La Peau de chagrin,* et dont le nom revient plus de trente fois dans son oeuvre. On peut apprécier tout particulièrement ici l'influence de Cuvier: le vocabulaire se fait 'scientifique' et le raisonnement a la rigueur d'une démonstration. Les deux termes 'déduction' et 'comparaison', destinés à mettre en lumière l'intérêt qu'offrent les descriptions, représentent, en outre, deux démarches essentielles de la méthode de Cuvier, que le romancier citait volontiers" ("Notes et variantes," 10:1580) ("We know the great admiration that Balzac had for the one whom he called 'the enchanter' in *La Peau de chagrin* and whose name appears more than thirty times in his work. We can especially

appreciate here the influence of Cuvier: vocabulary is made 'scientific' and the reasoning has the strength of a demonstration. The two terms, 'deduction' and 'comparison,' that are supposed to highlight the interest that descriptions offer, also represent two approaches essential to Cuvier's method that the novelist willingly cited").

19. In her extensive work on *La Recherche de l'absolu*, Fargeaud maintained that the representation of the house is "plus vraie que la nature, puisqu'elle synthétise tous les éléments de l'architecture flamande de l'extrême fin du XVIe siècle et du tout début du XVIIe siècle. 'L'esprit de la vieille Flandre', comme dit Balzac, revit vraiment en [sa description], et c'est bien là le fait de l'artiste. Il lui fallait situer cette maison dans une ville réelle, et nous avons vu qu'il avait sauvegardé pour l'essentiel la vraisemblance douaisienne. Mais le fait d'en avoir fait une maison typique lui garantissait du même coup une authenticité universellement flamande" *(Balzac et "La Recherche de l'absolu,"* p. 401) ("more true than nature because it synthesizes all the elements of Flemish architecture from the end of the sixteenth century and the beginning of the seventeenth. 'The spirit of old Flanders,' as Balzac says, lives again in [his description], and that is the doing of the artist. He had to situate the house in a real street, and we have seen that he had essentially safeguarded Douaisian verisimilitude. But by simply making the house a typical one he was guaranteed a universally Flemish authenticity at the same time").

20. Tzvetan Todorov, *Poétique de la prose*, p. 94.

21. Karel Kosik, *Die Dialektik des Konkreten* (Frankfurt, 1967), cited by Wolfgang Iser, "La Fiction en effet," p. 292.

22. Peter Brooks, *The Melodramatic Imagination, Balzac, Henry James, Melodrama, and the Mode of Excess*, p. 126.

23. Ibid., p. 125. The quotation from Albert Béquin is out of *Balzac lu et relu*, p. 49.

24. Fargeaud, *Balzac et "La Recherche de l'absolu,"* p. 370.

25. Brooks, *The Melodramatic Imagination*, p. 144.

26. Préface, *Histoire des Treize*, 5:791–92. All translations from this text are from *Ferragus: Chief of the Companions of Duty*, trans. Herbert J. Hunt (Harmondsworth, Middlesex, England: Penguin, 1974), pp. 21–153. This translation is from p. 26.

27. Rose Fortassier, Introduction, *Histoire des Treize*, 5:737–40. Although these three novels may once have been considered a trilogy, Cooper added two more Leatherstocking Tales, making five.

28. There are details in this four-page description of Paris that surely had more meaning for a nineteenth-century Parisian reader than they do for us today because of their cultural significance. Without the benefit of an excellent critical edition such as that prepared by Rose Fortassier for the 1977 Pléiade edition, we could not appreciate a few references in the description. I do not think, however, that a grasp of these details by the reader is essential to the successful functioning of the description, although, of course, it enhances reading enormously. Without it, we still receive the impressions of movement and force inscribed throughout the description. As is true throughout *La Comédie humaine*, Balzac was able to accommodate both the informed and the uninformed reader, while offering the former greater complexity. It is clear here that for readers of a time different from Balzac's own,

references to the reality of the author's world that were only superficially integrated into the narrative system are of less value than those rendered artistic by a more complete integration.

29. Balzac, "Lettres sur la littérature," p. 1062.

30. Balzac evoked the image of Paris as monster twice beyond the opening elaboration: "A Paris, les différents sujets qui concourent à la physionomie d'une portion quelconque de cette monstreuse cité s'harmonisent admirablement avec le caractère de l'ensemble" (5:866) ("In Paris, the different types contributing to the physiognomy of any portion of that monstrous city harmonize admirably with the character of the ensemble," p. 112); "Rien ne lui semblait plus naturel que d'anéantir ce receptacle de monstruosités" (5:891) ("Nothing seemed to him more natural than to annihilate this receptacle of monstrosities," p. 140).

Notes to Chapter IV
Mise en Abîme

1. Pierre Laubriet, *L'Intelligence de l'art chez Balzac*, pp. 143–44.

2. Martin Kanes called the actual reader an "enigmatic absence" as well as a "projection of aspects of the narrator's own consciousness," *Balzac's Comedy of Words*, p. 215.

3. Diana Festa McCormick, *Les Nouvelles de Balzac*, p. 9.

4. "La Grande Bretèche" was first published in 1832 under the title "Le Conseil," coupled with "Le Message" within the second volume of *Scènes de la vie privée*. In 1837, under the title "La Grande Bretèche ou les Trois Vengeances," it was combined with two other narrations and published in the third volume of *Etudes de Moeurs au dix-neuvième siècle*. In 1845, it was published separately in the fourth volume of *La Comédie humaine* but with the subtitle "fin d'Autre Etude de femme." Finally, in accordance with Balzac's directives, it was incorporated into that text in the Fürne corrigé. See the Introduction, 3:659–63. All translations of "La Grande Bretèche" used here are those of Sylvia Raphael (Harmondsworth, Middlesex, England: Penguin, 1977), pp. 176–95. Translations of the quotations from *Autre Etude de femme* are my own.

5. For readers familiar with Horace Bianchon it is not necessary to so establish him here. His identity as the humanist doctor, the bright and inquisitive young man of *Le Père Goriot*, or the established and wise physician of so many other texts is consistent throughout *La Comédie humaine*. Furthermore, he enjoys the reputation within this fictional world of a skillful raconteur, and Balzac frequently used him as narrator when a clever and sensitive narration was to be drawn. But the author did not rely upon the reader's familiarity with other texts and built into this one the credibility of Bianchon as narrator.

6. Obviously, the final scene can be interpreted as commentary on many things. Neither the moral implication of the story nor Balzac's use of the fantastic is pertinent to my subject of the relationship between the structure of the tale and our reading of it, although they are certainly most significant in the interpretation of *Autre Etude de femme*.

Notes to Chapter V
Mastery of *La Comédie humaine*

1. Fernand Lotte, "Le 'Retour des personnages' dans *La Comédie humaine: avantages et inconvénients du procédé*," p. 233.
2. Félix Davin, Introduction to *Etudes de Moeurs au XIXe siècle*, 1:1151.
3. Michel Butor, "Balzac et la réalité," pp. 83–84.
4. Ibid., p. 83.
5. In "On Presupposition and Narrative Strategy," Gerald Prince defines the presupposition of a statement as "the semantic element common to that statement, its negation, and its corresponding yes-no question" (p. 23). He uses this example: "John realizes that Peter's brother is intelligent." The sentence conveys the principal message that John has a high opinion of Peter's brother's level of intelligence. Beyond that message, however, is an implicit one, that Peter's brother is intelligent. The implicit message is the presupposition of the statement. One can expand on it by forming the question, "Is Peter's brother intelligent?"—the answer to which is, again, implicit in the original statement.
6. Maurice Bardèche, *Balzac romancier: La Formation de l'art du roman chez Balzac jusqu' à la publication du "Père Goriot,"* p. 524.
7. It is significant to note that in his texts Balzac, as an author acutely aware of his reading public, provided for the reader unfamiliar with the reappearing character and therefore oblivious to the implicit message that its presence communicates. Rare would be the case in which our failure to grasp an implicit message would prevent us from understanding the scene into which it is incorporated. The implicit message appeals to individual readers according to their experiences within *La Comédie humaine*. The more we read, therefore, the more rich with subtleties do the texts become. But the minimal text, the story on its own, will be available to each reader.
8. Wolfgang Iser, *The Act of Reading: A Theory of Aesthetic Response*, p. 97. The full discussion of these concepts is found in pages 97–103.
9. Ibid., p. 97.
10. Ibid., pp. 100–3.
11. Wolfgang Iser, "Indeterminacy and the Reader's Response in Prose Fiction," p. 43.
12. For a detailed discussion of the significance of the blank space, see Iser, *The Act of Reading*, pp. 197–203.
13. Iser, "Indeterminacy and the Reader's Response," p. 14.
14. Despite the care with which these characters were obviously created, some inconsistency can be found. Many errors are of a chronological nature (a character reappears who has in fact died in another text) or involve an unlikely transformation of physical appearance (see Lotte, "Le 'Retour des personnages' "). These inconsistencies do not seriously impair our grasp of characters or our active participation in their development, however. In fact, it is my experience that we compensate for or correct the inconsistencies as we read.
15. Lotte, p. 234.
16. Of course it is the frequent repetition of the character's essential qualities that allows us gradually to see Bianchon as symbolizing these traits in Balzac's world. At the same time, the repetition of what is essential is a means by which Balzac accommodated at each appearance of the character the reader who has not yet encountered him.

17. Honoré de Balzac, *Le Père Goriot,* trans. Henry Reed (New York: New American Library, Signet Classics, 1962), pp. 135–36. All English references to *Le Père Goriot* are from this translation.

18. Honoré de Balzac, *Illusions perdues,* trans. Herbert J. Hunt (Harmondsworth, Middlesex, England: Penguin, 1971), p. 216. All English references to *Illusions perdues* are from this translation.

19. This passage represents yet another pair of audiences who receive this tale, those who see *Valentine* at the Gymnase-Dramatique, and the guests at the château d'Anzy. The passage complicates in retrospect or in advance the structure of "La Grande Bretèche" with its *mise en abîme* of the narrator-narrataire axis.

20. This is a particularly interesting passage because it invites the reader to involve at least four other narrations in the reading of *Le Lys dans la vallée:* the "noble Juana" is found in *Les Marana* (10:1037–94); Madame d'Aiglemont and her husband in *La Femme de trente ans* (2:463–504); the Marquis and the Marquise d'Espard in *L'Interdiction* (3:421–93). In one passage, then, Balzac offered a challenge to his reader to grasp the relationship of four tales to *Le Lys dans la vallée,* creating a category of narration. The passage serves not only to join these texts in an obvious way (but a joining that only the reader can do), but also to enhance the reading of *Le Lys dans la vallée* with the embellishment that these detours provide.

21. Jean-Luis Bourget, "Balzac et le déchiffrement des signes," p. 73.

22. Ibid., p. 84.

23. Obviously, a great many readers now know that Carlos Herrera of *Illusions perdues* is the Vautrin of *Le Père Goriot* before they ever encounter him. Unfortunately for many a twentieth-century reader, the strategy that Balzac incorporated into his presentation may be less effective because of the popularity of the character.

24. Balzac first identified the character not by using his name but by reference to the story recounted in *Illusions perdues* of his unsuccessful love affair with Mme de Bargeton. The reference to that text, then, prepares us to associate the masked character with Carlos Herrera and reminds us of its unresolved ending.

25. Lotte, p. 223.

26. Honoré de Balzac, *A Study in Feminine Psychology,* trans. Sylvia Raphael (Harmondsworth, Middlesex, England: Penquin, 1977), p. 72.

BIBLIOGRAPHY

I. Primary

Balzac, Honoré de. *La Comédie humaine*. Edited by Pierre-Georges Castex. 12 vols. Bibliothèque de la Pléïade. Paris: Gallimard, 1976–1981.

———. *Correspondance*. Edited by Roger Pierrot. 5 vols. Paris: Garnier, 1960–1969.

———. *Lettres à Madame Hanska*. Edited by Roger Pierrot. 4 vols. Paris: Les Bibliophiles de l'Originale, 1967–1968.

———. "Lettres sur la littérature." In *Oeuvres complètes de Honoré de Balzac*. Vol. 40, pp. 271–329. Paris: Louis Conard, 1940.

———. "Notes philosophiques." In *Oeuvres complètes*. Vol. 25. Paris: Club de l'honnête homme, 1962.

II. Secondary

a. On *La Comédie humaine*

Bardèche, Maurice. *Balzac, romancier: La Formation de l'art du roman chez Balzac jusqu'à la publication du "Pere Goriot."* Paris: Plon, 1940.

Barthes, Roland. *S/Z*. Paris: Seuil, 1970.

Bellos, David. *Balzac Criticism in France, 1850–1900: The Making of a Reputation*. Oxford: Clarendon Press, 1976.

———. "Balzac, Stendhal et le public à l'epoque du réalisme." In *Stendhal-Balzac: réalisme et cinéma: Actes du XIe Congrès international stendhalien, Auxerre, 1976*, edited by Victor del Litto, pp. 29–36. Grenoble: Presses universitaires de Grenoble, 1978.

Béquin, Albert. *Balzac lu et relu*. Paris: Seuil, 1965.

Bourget, Jean-Luis. "Balzac et le déchiffrement des signes." *L'Année balzacienne 1977*, pp. 74–89.

Brombert, Victor. "Nathalie: ou, Le lecteur caché de Balzac." In *Mouvements premiers: Etudes critiques offertes à Georges Poulet*, pp. 177–90. Paris: José Corti, 1972.

Brooks, Peter. "Balzac: Melodrama and Metaphor." *The Hudson Review* 22 (1969):213–28.

———. *The Melodramatic Imagination, Balzac, Henry James, Melodrama, and the Mode of Excess*. New Haven and London: Yale University Press, 1976.

Butor, Michel. "Balzec et la réalité." *Répertoire, études et confér-
ences, 1948–1959*, pp. 79–93. Paris: Minuit, 1960.

Canfield, Arthur Graves. *The Reappearing Character in Balzac's
"Comédie Humaine."* Chapel Hill: University of North Carolina
Press, 1961.

Dargan, Edwin Preston, ed. *Studies in Balzac's Realism.* 2d ed. 1932.
Reprint. New York: Russell and Russell, 1967.

[Davin, Félix.] Introduction to *Etudes de Moeurs au XIXè siècle. La
Comédie humaine*, 1:1145–72.

Delattre, Geneviève. *Les Opinions littéraires de Balzac.* Paris:
Presses universitaires de France, 1961.

Fargeaud, Madeleine. *Balzec et "La Recherche de l'Absolu."* Paris:
Hachette, 1968.

Frappier-Mazur, Lucienne. *L'Expression métaphorique dans "La
Comédie humaine."* Paris: Klincksieck, 1976.

Imbert, Patrick. *Sémiotique et description balzacienne.* Ottawa:
Editions de l'Université d'Ottawa, 1978.

Jacques, Georges. *Paysages et structures dans "La Comédie humaine."*
Louvain: Presses universitaires de Louvain, 1975.

Kanes, Martin. *Balzac's Comedy of Words.* Princeton: Princeton
University Press, 1975.

Laubriet, Pierre. *L'Intelligence de l'art chez Balzac, D'Une esthétique
balzacienne.* Paris: Didier, 1961.

Lotte, Fernand. "Le 'Retour des Personnages' dans *La Comédie
humaine:* avantages et inconvénients du procédé." *L'Année
balzacienne 1961*, pp. 227–81.

Mayer, Gilbert. *La Qualification affective dans les romans d'Honoré
de Balzac.* Paris: Droz, 1940.

Mazat, Léo. "Récit(s) dans le récit: L'échange du récit chez Balzac."
L'Année balzacienne 1976, pp. 129–61.

McCormick, Diana Festa. *Les Nouvelles de Balzac.* Paris: Librairie
Nizet, 1973.

Prendergast, Christopher. *Balzac, Fiction and Melodrama.* New York:
Holmes and Meier Publishers, 1978.

Richard, Jean-Pierre. *Etudes sur le romantisme.* Paris: Seuil, 1970.

Thérien, Michel. "Métaphores animales et écriture balzaciennes:
le portrait et la description." *L'Année balzacienne 1979*, pp. 193–208.

Vannier, Bernard. *L'Inscription du corps: Pour une sémiotique du
portrait balzacien.* Paris: Klincksieck, 1972.

——— . "Jeux du texte balzacien." *Europe*, October, 1970, pp. 167–81.

Yücel, Tahsin. *Figures et messages dans "La Comédie humaine."*
Tours: Mame, 1972.

b. Theory

Alter, Robert. *Partial Magic: The Novel as a Self-Conscious Genre.*

Berkeley and Los Angeles: University of California Press, 1975.

Barthes, Roland. "L'Effet du réel." *Communications 11* (1968):84–89.

Beardsley, Monroe C. "The Metaphorical Twist." *Philosophy and Phenomenological Research* 22 (1962):293–307.

Bleich, David. "The Determination of Literary Value." *Literature and Psychology* 17 (1967):19–30.

——— . *Readings and Feelings: An Introduction to Subjective Criticism*. Urbana: National Council of Teachers of English, 1975.

——— . "The Subjective Character of Critical Interpretation." *College English* 36 (1975):739–55.

——— . *Subjective Criticism*. Baltimore: Johns Hopkins University Press, 1978.

——— . "The Subjective Paradigm in Science, Psychology and Criticism." *New Literary History* 7 (1976):313–34.

Booth, Wayne C. *The Rhetoric of Fiction*. Chicago: University of Chicago Press, 1961.

Brombert, Victor. "Opening Signals in Narrative." *New Literary History* 11 (1980):489–502.

Coquet, Jean-Claude. "La Relation sémantique sujet-objet." *Langages* 31 (1973):80–89.

Eco, Umberto. *The Role of the Reader: Explorations in the Semiotics of Texts*. Bloomington and London: Indiana University Press, 1979.

Fish, Stanley. "Literature in the Reader: Affective Stylistics." *New Literary History* 2 (1970):123–62.

Frappier-Mazur, Lucienne. "La Description mnémonique dans le roman romantique." *Littérature*, no. 38 (1980), pp. 3–26.

Freud, Sigmund. *The Standard Edition of the Complete Psychological Works of Sigmund Freud*. Translated and edited by James Strachey. 24 vols. London: Hogarth Press and the Institute for Psycho-analysis, 1953–1974.

Genette, Gérard. *Figures III*. Paris: Seuil, 1972.

——— . "Frontières du récit." *Figures II*. Paris: Seuil, 1969.

Gombrich, E. H. *Art and Illusion*. Princeton: Princeton University Press, 1960.

Hamon, Philippe. "Qu'est-ce que c'est qu'une description?" *Poétique* 12 (1972):465–85.

Henle, Paul, ed. *Language, Thought and Culture*. Ann Arbor: University of Michigan Press, 1972.

Holland, Norman N. *The Dynamics of Literary Response*. New York: Oxford University Press, 1968.

——— . *5 Readers Reading*. New Haven: Yale University Press, 1975.

——— . "The New Paradigm: Subjective or Transactive?" *New Literary History* 7 (1976):335–46.

Iser, Wolfgang. *The Act of Reading: A Theory of Aesthetic Response*. Baltimore and London: Johns Hopkins University Press, 1978.

BIBLIOGRAPHY

———. "La Fiction en effet." *Poétique* 19 (1979):275–98.

———. *The Implied Reader, Patterns of Communication in Prose Fiction from Bunyan to Beckett.* Baltimore and London: Johns Hopkins University Press, 1974.

———. "Indeterminacy and the Reader's Response in Prose Fiction." In *Aspects of Narrative,* edited by J. Hillis Miller, pp. 1–45. New York: Columbia University Press, 1971.

Jakobson, Roman. "Deux Aspects du langage et deux types d'aphasies." In *Essais de linguistique générale,* pp. 43–67. Paris: Seuil, 1963.

LeGuern, Michel. *Sémantique de la métaphore et de la métonymie.* Paris: Librairie Larousse, 1973.

Lesser, Simon O. *Fiction and the Unconscious.* 2d ed. 1957. Reprint. New York: Vintage Books, 1962.

Naumann, Manfred. "Literary Production and Reception." *New Literary History* 8 (1976):107–26.

Ong, Walter J. "The Writer's Audience is Always a Fiction." *PMLA* 90 (1975):9–21.

Prince, Gerald. "Introduction à l'étude du narrataire." *Poétique* 14 (1973): 178–96.

———. "Notes Towards a Categorization of Fictional 'Narratees'." *Genre* 4 (1971):100–5.

———. "On Presupposition and Narrative Strategy." *Centrum* 1 (1973):23–31.

Richards, I. A. *Practical Criticism.* London: Routledge & Kegan Paul, 1929.

Ricoeur, Paul. *La Métaphore vive.* Paris: Seuil, 1975.

Riffaterre, Michael. "La Métaphore filée dans la poésie surréaliste." *Langue française,* September 1969, pp. 46–60.

Sacks, Sheldon, ed. *On Metaphor.* Chicago: University of Chicago Press, 1979.

Todorov, Tzvetan. *Poétique de la prose.* Paris: Seuil, 1971.

Wellek, René, and Warren, Austin. *Theory of Literature.* New York: Harcourt, Brace and World, 1956.

Williams, D. A., ed. *The Monster in the Mirror: Studies in Nineteenth-Century Realism.* Oxford and New York: Oxford University Press, 1978.

Wimsatt, W. K., Jr., and Beardsley, Monroe C. *The Verbal Icon.* Lexington: University of Kentucky Press, 1954.

INDEX